D1525363

RECIPES FOR A GREAT LIFE

The Book That Will Fire You Up, Feed Your Soul, and Make You Feel Good

BY

BRUCE JEPPESEN

Ordering Information: Quantity sales. Special discounts are available on quantity purchases by corporations, associations, and others. Orders by U.S. trade bookstores and wholesalers.

DREAMSTARTERS

www.DreamStartersPublishing.com

Table of Contents

Foreword by Tony Whatley

There is a too much unnecessary pain in this world. Our society has become conditioned to live with physical and emotional pain, while displaying a smile to conceal it. It doesn't have to be this way.

I've been in a low point, before. The year was 2000 for me, but it feels like yesterday in my memories. At the time, I was broke financially, physically, and mentally. Every day seemed to be on repeat, with no real awareness of time passing. Each day I dreaded waking up, as I knew it would just be another day of suffering. That depression lasted nearly two years, and I felt like I was at the bottom of a deep hole with a spoon to dig myself out.

I felt like my life was spiraling out of control. Up until that period of my life, things generally were progressing as planned. I had just graduated college. I had no debt. I was excited about the future, and had a positive outlook. Then everything changed in 2000. I became the father of a newborn son, but had a failed and toxic relationship with his mother. No matter how much I tried to make it work, it only grew worse. It was literally the worst relationship I have ever been in. I felt trapped. I had lost my engineering job six months earlier, due to an industry downturn. This put me $40,000 in debt because

4

I had to live off of credit cards. I didn't have much experience, and nobody was hiring. Eventually I found another low-paying role, but even that wasn't enough to pay my bills and debt down.

I made the hardest decision in my life; I left that relationship with my son's mother. I could not remain with someone who laughed at my dreams, and kept me in a negative emotional state. The day I took action to leave that relationship, I still recall the stress dissipating as I drove out that morning to go find my own apartment. I started to feel lighter and saw a glimmer of hope. It was as if I started to see in color, again.

I've always been fully accountable for my situations in life, so I focused on getting to work. I had to work three jobs, for three years, just to get back to zero. I started my first online business in 2001, which eventually grew into the most successful within its category, eventually earning me millions by age 34.

None of this positive shift would have occurred, had I simply settled, or remained within an unhappy and unsupported life. I had to force a change. I had to take back control over my life. I had to be okay with the results and opinions of others, which are always beyond my control. I became hyper-focused only on actions within my control.

When I first met Bruce Jeppesen, I could sense that he had a story buried inside of himself. He was holding back, despite his physical strength and size. They often say that the most silent person in the room, likely has the most to say; but they tend to remain silent. That was Bruce.

I knew we had to help him bring his story to the world. Our group of entrepreneurs could see the potential within him that he didn't see in himself. We encouraged him to participate in our group challenges, and he didn't hesitate. Bruce has so much wisdom inside him, and he knew that he had to make some changes in order to evolve and improve his situation.

It's been an inspiring journey to witness Bruce, as he continues to improve, inspire, and educate others. This is what makes him the perfect person to deliver the message within this book. His story will relate with millions of you that want to overcome adversity, and perhaps get out of your own way.

Let's get your fire started and get to cooking.

Tony Whatley

Best-Selling Author, Keynote Speaker, Business Coach

Introduction

My life has been full of many different journeys, and has presented me with many challenges and wonderful opportunities. It took a lot of effort to create a life that I'm fully satisfied with and I feel like I have to give part of that credit to my grandparents. You hardly ever hear people talk about what their grandparents used to do and how that affects them now in adulthood, but I know that I can thank my grandparents for bringing me where I am now.

When I was really young, I lived close to both of my grandmothers, so I would see them very frequently. I used to go to each of their houses visit with and watch them cook up a storm for the family. Women from that generation were really good cooks and made many amazing, meals out of almost nothing. They had learned to do that during the tough economic times of the Great Depression and World War II.

I remember just sitting in a chair right beside the stove and watching my grandmother's cook. Talking with them and visiting them was one of the highlights of my life at that young age, and this was especially true because of how hard life could be outside of that little bubble.

My family had its share of struggles, but food always brought us together. Sometimes, when I came home from school, my mom would be cooking bread and just the smell of fresh bread wafting through the air was enough to make a bad day better. I always loved seeing rolls and loaves of bread fresh out of the oven on the kitchen table.

I eventually also learned how to cook after watching my grandmothers and my mom too. I had to learn to cook out of necessity since as I got older, family meals came fewer and farther in between.

My immediate family is mostly gone now, but what I learned from them remains. Just like how the smell of fresh bread brings back some good memories, I believe that food can help people create new positive memories and connect with one another. Helping people connect with their community and with each other through food is a passion of mine, but it took a long time for me to get to that point.

This book for me is an exploration of the lessons I've learned throughout life and how they've brought me to this moment. I learned so much, and so much stuck with me through childhood, but it took a lot of work for me to start wanting to be part of a larger community and sharing my talent for cooking. This book talks about all of the ways I learned and grew throughout my life and I hope that you can take these lessons and apply them to your own life. As a cool way to teach a lesson, I combine each lesson with my favorite dishes. If you can feed your mind and stomach at the same time, then you are well on your way to great life. Enjoy!

Chapter One

A Journey to Self-Love

I feel like self-love is an excellent start to this book, just because of its importance. We often go through life not really knowing how to love ourselves, and that lack of love can be so very detrimental to who we are and what we want to do. I often wonder how my own life might have been different if I had learned to love myself at an earlier age, but I didn't get there until late in my life. It's never too late to love yourself, and it's never too late to learn to be kind to yourself. In this chapter, I want to tell you my story and remind you of three things: You are good enough, kind enough, and strong enough to take back your life.

You are Good Enough

It seems like a simple enough phrase, but understanding and accepting that I was good enough took a lot of work because, for the longest time, I didn't believe it. Why would I? I listened to far too many people telling me that I wasn't good enough, wasn't worthy enough, that I struggled to turn around and yell back, "Yes, I am good enough."

Growing up in rural Montana was challenging. My family was pretty tight-knit. We were raised fairly strictly, and not really allowed to have much of an opinion. If we were told to do something, we were never allowed to talk back. My siblings and I were raised to be seen,but rarelyheard.

Not being able to speakup as a child at home was frustrating, but was even more difficult once I started my school years in a small country school. I eventually moved to a larger school in the nearby town. Going to school in a new town showed me, for the first time, how people could be cruel for no reason. The kids in school taught me many lessons like I wasn't good enough. Not good enough for friendship, not good enough for class, not good enough for opinions, just not good enough. And as a voiceless kid, I believed it all. I kept on believing and grew up to be a voiceless adult. It wasn't until much later, decades later, that I learned I had a voice and that I was good enough to use it.

I guess it all came to a head in my 40s. By this point, I was struggling. It's hard to go through life and not really take power over it since I was busy listening to everyone else instead of finding my own voice. Depression hit me hard, and it was a constant companion. During this time, I was working for a company with a real jerk of a coworker. This was a guy who knew how to play the game and stay out of trouble. Anytime the bosses were gone, he would treat everyone else like garbage. Any complaints made to supervisors were met with absolutely no changes. We were basically told, "Tough shit." So I started to feel not only voiceless but powerless. Powerless to make changes or to help. Voiceless, powerless, and not good enough. Worthless.

What a potent cocktail of agony. These three thoughts and emotions helped my feelings of depression to explode. I felt low, lower than I had felt in a very long time, and with those intense feelings came feelings of life not being worth it. I started thinking about suicide and how, when it was time, I would just end it.

On one incredibly tough day, I decided that this was the day. This was the day I was going to end it. I was 43 years old and ready for it to be over. On my drive home, I was thinking about suicide and ending it. But then, I thought about my dog. I had this fantastic dog at the time, and I realized that he wouldn't understand what had happened if I didn't return home. He would just be there waiting for me, not realizing that I wasn't coming home. Picturing him waiting patiently for me made me pause. I couldn't do that to him.

12

Instead of choosing to die, I turned my car into the parking lot of a local church. I figured I might be able to talk with a pastor and maybe this guy could help me. I think I was fortunate to turn into that church that day. The pastor welcomed me in, sat down with me, and just talked with me. He had a way with words, and we talked and talked. Finally, he said to me, "Let God help you." And I decided, why not? It's not like I had any other options. Afterward, I went home and hugged my dog. He literally saved my life that day, and for probably the first time in my life, I decided to control what I was going through with my mental health.

For a while, I went to a psychiatrist who put me on some medication, but it didn't help. Still feeling down but wanting to make a change, I reached out to a psychologist my dad had known for years. This was a guy who I had heard about and knew was a good guy. So I took the time and went to go visit him. I walked into his office lobby and sat there to wait. He came out to get me, and we sat down in his office. The first thing he told me was, "I've got to tell you. I've been doing this for 33 years, and when I walked out to the lobby to get you, you were the saddest looking person I'd ever seen". He didn't say it as a statement about my clothing choices, or my physical appearance, but about my expression and body language. It was the first time I realized just how noticeable my sadness was. Looking back on it, I didn't believe I was good enough for positive things to happen in my life. That negativity kept me a prisoner for an awfully long time.

It took a lot of work, but I slowly started to make changes to help me find my voice, my power, and my worth. The pastor and my psychologist both really helped me find those things in my life. I went to church, found new hobbies, and made friends. I also made an exit plan for leaving that toxic work environment, and while I didn't have a lot of money, I chose to go anyway.

It took time. Healing from mental wounds is a long process and learning to find your own worth is an even longer process, but I had a lot of support to help me get there. Many years after that, I met and visited with an amazing woman, Susanne Zavelle who shared her story which was very similar to mine. The way she talked about it really stuck with me, especially how she took control of her life to make it what she wanted it to be. I wanted to do the same thing in my life. A week after she shared her story, I sat down in my home and told myself, "I am good enough." I wrote it down on a little card. "I am good enough." And for the first time, I actually believed it. "I am good enough." It was January 2020.
You are good enough.

You are Kind Enough

During my healing process, one of my first lessons was learning how to be kind to myself. While I gave myself good food and sometimes went on vacation, being good to myself really meant being kind to myself. I lacked that level of self-love, and I honestly didn't know how to get it. For years, people would ask me why I was so down on myself. They would tell me to speak more positively to myself. Still, nobody likes to be told what to do, especially after spending such a long time listening to what others wanted and ignoring my own voice. I would get mad at them and mad at myself, but they were right. I was down on myself, but I didn't know how to stop it. I didn't know how to love myself. Self-kindness was a foreign language to me, and it wasn't something I even knew how to practice.

I was unkind to myself every day. If I was cooking something and it didn't turn out good, my automatic thoughts would tell me how stupid I was and that I couldn't do anything right. I said these phrases all throughout my life. I was stuck on repeat and had no way to skip forward. If something wasn't perfect the first time I did it, I told myself that I was a worthless loser.

It wasn't until someone talked to me out of compassion and love that I started to realize how my negativity affected myself and others. My cousin, Kenny Jeppesen, who is like a brother to me, one day stopped me and said, "You know, I'm not saying you're negative, but you don't really talk positive." He said it in an entirely judgment freeway. It was spoken with empathy, and it got to me more than when other people would tell me the exact same thing. He was kind enough to point out my negativity in a way I wasn't used to. It changed my perspective and gave me the necessary push to start changing.

They say that the first thought that goes through your head is the one you're conditioned to. The second thought is the one that defines you. I guess for me, my first thoughts were simply echoes of the words thrown at me by people and some of the students in my school. I learned to feel worthless, and I accepted that feeling every time I put myself down. I had to learn to change the narrative with my second thought, the one that defines me.

Not too long ago, I was at a meeting trying to network and talk with people. I had a new phone and was seriously struggling with it. I just couldn't get it to work the way I was used to with my old phones, and with each person I talked to, I would say that I was sorry, I'm not a techie person, as I tried to enter their phone numbers. After about the fifth time of doing this song and dance, I realized that I was speaking down to myself. Sure, it wasn't as bad as how I used to speak to myself, but it was still a little unkind. It's not that I wasn't a techie person, but that I just hadn't learned how to use this phone yet. Yet. Using that word helps remind me that I can improve and I can learn. I just haven't *yet*. Switching to this mindset was one of the most significant changes I made for myself. My first thought was a little unkind, but once I was aware of it, I changed the thought into something better.

Talking down to ourselves, being unkind, is called negative self-talk. While it can sometimes propel us to do better, it mostly puts us in a negative mindset. And if we repeat those phrases over and over again, they become our standard. Negativity becomes our first thought. Suddenly, negativity starts to bleed into other areas of our lives and our perceptions of reality. Our brains tend to see or hear something and filter it to fit our perceptions. If we're really negative to ourselves, then it doesn't matter what people say to us, we'll always see it through a negative lens. Negativity feeds on negativity. But if we change our mindset, change our self-talk, then we can change our perceptions. If our negative self-talk becomes positive self-talk, or self-kindness, then we can start to see kindness in other areas of our lives as well.

For me, this meant that I worked on stopping my negativity and including some more positivity. If I said, "I'm so stupid," I would turn it around and instead say, "I don't know how to do this yet, but I'm learning," or, "I don't get this right now, but I'll improve." If you're also struggling with negative self-talk, then the most powerful thing you can do for yourself is to turn your negative into a positive. All of a sudden, you'll start to think a little happier, walk a little taller, and start to have more confidence in what you can do. You'll also find yourself drifting more towards people who have a similar mindset.

You are worthy of self-kindness and love. You are worthy of positivity in your life. I am worthy of kindness. You are worthy of kindness. We are worth enough.

You are Strong Enough

No one can make you feel inferior without your consent." Eleanor Roosevelt famously said this, and I really wish I had understood it when I was younger. Unfortunately, as a child, I didn't take this advice to heart and instead let people tell me who I was and what I could do. I internalized their words and accepted it as fact, allowing it to hurt me over and over again until I was left with nothing. It was like death by a thousand cuts, each one small but as a whole, devastating. And all because I let peoples words hurt me.

Yes, words hurt. People can saythings ,yell at you and criticize you. But the moment we accept their words as the truth of who we are, that hurt becomes more permanent. It becomes a part of our identity and our stories to ourselves. We start to repeat it because that's what we understand about ourselves. We let ourselves feel inferior, all because of someone else's words. We give them the power to tell us who we are and what we are worth. No one deserves that power but you. No one deserves that power over me except me.

So take that power back. You're strong enough. I'm strong enough. We don't have to let other people's words mean more to us than what we think about ourselves. We don't have to let their hurtful words imprint on us and cut our souls. When the hurt comes, and it will, we can experience it and then choose not to agree. We can choose to counter the damage with our own self-kindness, our own love. We can take back our power.

Sometimes, it's hard to notice when someone's negative words bring you down, when their comments and criticisms are hurting you. At first, it's just small things, but over time, all of those tiny cuts start to hurt more and more until finally, you realize that you've been bleeding this whole time, and it's time to stop. That's the point where you know you can't take it anymore. You can't take this person's negativity towards you. So you then have two choices: you can choose to stand up for yourself and start to take back your power by reminding yourself of the good things you are, that you're worthy and that you're good enough. Or you could choose to let them keep hurting you until there's nothing left. Choose the first option.

Eleanor Roosevelt left us with another beautiful reminder: "You gain strength, courage, and confidence by every experience in which you really stop to look fear in the face. You are able to say to yourself, 'I lived through this horror. I can take the next thing that comes along."

You've lived through the hurt. You gain strength by reminding yourself of your worth. And every time you have to deal with the pain, it will get easier. You've lived through it, so you can take the next thing that happens. You are strong enough.

Connecting Lessons with Food

Bacon wrapped Asparagus

Ingredients:

- Fresh Asparagus
- Peppered bacon
- Your favorite cooking oil
- Your seasonings of choice

Rinse, drain and cut off the thicker parts of each stem then pat dry

Take 4-5 pieces of Asparagus and bunch up then wrap with 1 or 2 pieces of bacon according to the size of the bacon strip.

Rub each bunch lightly with oil and add seasonings.

Cook until bacon is done and Asparagus is tender.

Remove from heat and serve immediately

This goes great with any meat I have tried it with.

Note- I have found that the thinner the Asparagus the faster and easier it cooks and tastes better. The thick heavy stalks are bitter in my experience.

Chapter Two

Take That First Step

It's hard to take a step to change your life in a new direction. For me, it was tremendously difficult. Now, it's not as though my whole life was difficult but during those times when things were rough, it was hard to take a step to make a change. This was especially true when I was depressed working at that terrible job. I had the voices of everyone else, including my own, telling me that I wasn't good enough to make a change.

Being knocked down by everyone around me, and by myself, made it doubly hard to stand myself back up again. But I had to take that first step to make a change and for me, I couldn't take that step until I felt like I had hit rock bottom. Take my advice and start before you hit that point.

Back then, I tended to throw myself into new things, and new experiences. I knew it wouldn't turn out perfect, but I just wanted to get it done and if it wasn't perfect, because nothing new is, it was just a reflection of my worth, according to my negative state of mind. When things didn't work out, I would hesitate to make any more changes, or try something new. But something had to change for me. Something had to get better, and it wasn't going to be my outside experiences. It had to start with me and my internal beliefs.

It took a change in my mindset, the feeling of hopelessness, for me to take that first step. But really, changing your mindset from feeling like you're worthless into being worth enough to be loved and happy, is what you need to take the first step. It doesn't have to be a huge step, but it does need to be a step.

Changing our Mindset

Everything that people tell us as we grow up influences how we think about ourselves. We can start telling ourselves the same stories and truly believe that we're just like what our parents or peers told us. You already read what my story was in the previous chapter, but take a moment to think about what your story is. What were you taught about yourself as you grew up and do you still echo those stories now?

23

The way we think about ourselves, whether positive or negative teaches us how to act in our lives. When I thought I was unworthy or not enough, it affected what I did and made it hard to make any changes in my life. I knew things had to change. I knew. I just didn't have the right mindset to make that change, to take that first step.

We have to change our mindsets in order to drive us forward to do what we need or want to do and at the same time, we have to change the story we tell about ourselves. When I was in a bad spot, I didn't believe that I could make a change and that I could only do what I was talented to do. So if something didn't work out when I tried it, it was because I didn't have the talent for it. But what I needed to think was that it was just a skill I hadn't yet developed.

My first mindset was called a fixed mindset, one that depended on my personal skill, rather than one that depended on growth and learning. A fixed mindset isn't one we can keep if we want to take our first step. It's not one we can keep if we want to make a change in our lives, and it wasn't one I could keep once I decided to start making a change.

Making a change was a risk and had its own set of challenges. I had to learn to create a new self-image, but also learn to be kinder to myself. I had to learn that I was worthy enough to get better and then actually take the steps to get better. With all of these things I had to do, a fixed mindset would have made me give up when faced with the challenges. If I chose to believe that the only way my life could get better was through the work of others, whether that was my co-worker quitting his job, or people treating me better, then my life wouldn't change. After all, I can't control what other people do or say, and so if they don't change, am I supposed to sit there and suffer?

A fixed mindset means believing that things outside of my control have to be perfect for everything in my life to be perfect. It also meant that if things didn't work out, it was okay to quit and move on to other things. I gave up when challenges came up and if I made a mistake with something, I wouldn't learn how to fix it or improve myself. With a fixed mindset, I was successful at the things I really tried or the things I had the skill set for, but over the years, when things were out of my control or things got very difficult, I had a hard time facing the challenge and growing from it.

When I was a young adult, I joined the military, simply because I didn't have anything else to do. I wasn't satisfied with seasonal work or with work in Montana, and the military was my second escape, to leave behind problems in Montana and find something else to do. Then, when I left the military, I didn't know what to do. So instead of approaching my problems and trying to solve them, I returned to what I knew: life in Montana. I eventually ran again. So when things

25

became difficult for me, when the going got tough, I quit. It's what I did throughout my whole life. I would move on when something wasn't going right for me.

But it turns out that unsolved problems tend to follow you wherever you go. They don't just disappear because you ran away from them. If my problem was being dissatisfied with my life, just moving to a new place wasn't going to change that. I had to address the roots of the problem before I could fix the problem. However, because I only ran as my way of problem-solving, nothing was really solved.

A fixed mindset set me up to not grow as I need to. It set me up to continue patterns in my life, instead of learning and changing to fit the circumstances around me. What I needed instead was a mindset that would help me grow.

It wasn't easy and it took a very long time to change my mindset, but I eventually gained one that helped me grow and develop. It helped me learn that I am capable of making changes and facing challenges. I am capable of growing from failure and mistakes, just like you are. This mindset is called a growth mindset. With a growth mindset, experiencing a mistake or failure isn't the end of the road. It's just a lesson to be learned and a sign that I'm not there yet, but I can get there through hard work. It's just like I mentioned earlier; I may not be perfect or get things done well but it just means I have room to improve and that I will, eventually, get it.

26

A mindset like this helped me realize that while I might not be the best at something, I can still continue to grow. Growth mindsets set us up for reaching our goals and facing challenges. It even helps us solve problems, develop creativity, and develop our skills through hard work. What a growth mindset means for me is that, yeah, things might be difficult, but I can get through it and keep working hard to get where I want to go.

When cooking, if I'm trying to make gravy for the first time, I'm going to struggle a little. Even with a written recipe, if I've never made something before, it's not always going to be easy from the get-go. With a fixed mindset, if I messed up the gravy, I would be incredibly frustrated and eventually give up. I might do something else that I've already mastered and avoid making gravy in the future. But that would mean that I'm not learning something from the mistakes I made. A fixed mindset in this situation means that I wouldn't be confident enough to try again, even though I might fail.

However, if I'm making gravy with a growth mindset, I'll still face the same struggles, but instead of giving up, maybe I'll take the time to go through the recipe again and see where I made mistakes. I can analyze what I need to do differently, and try again. Sure, I'll probably throw out that batch, but I won't stop making gravy altogether. I'll keep practicing and trying until I get it. A growth mindset in this situation means that I'll grow in both skill level and confidence when I do eventually succeed, because I will eventually succeed with enough practice.

The thing is, that in nearly everything, we can succeed with enough hard work and perseverance. But we have to have the right mindset to get us there. Luckily, our thought processes aren't set in stone. I mean, in my own life I spent a large majority of it having negative thoughts about my skills or abilities, but eventually, I was able to change my perspective and change my mindset. We are all resilient and that means that we are capable of surviving tough times, while also growing from that experience. We can very quickly adapt in the way we need to. We just have to set ourselves up to succeed by first believing that we can, in fact, succeed.

Even if you're in a low place like I was, take the time to slowly start changing your mindset and one of the greatest ways to do this is through a dose of self-love. Your support group can help you with this, but you also have to accept that there are some parts of yourself that are pretty great. It took me a while to get there, and eventually, you'll get there too. An easy way to do this is to catch yourself saying negative things about yourself. If you can catch that negative thought, then you can follow it up with a second, more loving thought. In the first chapter I talked about how I'm not stupid, I just haven't figured this thing out yet. For me, using this

28

explanation is a little way to add more self-love to my life. It helps keep my negativity down and increases my self-confidence. It also helps to support my growth mindset. So give that a little try.

When you start to make little changes to your mindset, you're going to always have setbacks. After all, it's a hard process and if we've lived our whole lives with a poor opinion of ourselves or our abilities, then change won't be a simple thing. But we have to keep trying. We have to keep trying to support ourselves and love ourselves and grow from our mistakes. We have to be persistent and sometimes a little additional help can go a long way.

For me, relying on my faith, my pastor, my friends, really helped me create this environment where I could be okay with failure. It helped set me up for a mindset of belief in myself. It also set up a more loving mindset for me too. So if you find yourself struggling to make that first, little change with your mindset, then think about getting some outside help. There are people out there who would happily help you through the process and prop you up when you need a little boost.

While you can work with your support group, also start to find strategies to help you develop your skills. If you have problems that are bringing you down, then learn to explore the problem. Try and find different ways to solve it before you consider quitting the problem. Start trying new things, even if it feels like a risk, because trying new things will slowly give you confidence in your ability to solve your problems. Solving problems will start to help you build your growth mindset, instead of giving up and continuing to follow the patterns you had before. As you try new things, you will fail, and that's totally ok! We all fail sometimes. What matters is trying again using a different way, or learning from the mistakes we made. Don't just give up.

How to Take that First Step

The first step in my growth mindset was realizing that I could get better, that my depression and life circumstances didn't have to control everything in my life. I didn't have to give up on life just because things were difficult right now. I could work through it, though I needed help and support to get there. I could make myself happy so long as I tried to solve the problems in my life and start actively repairing what needed to be fixed. However, since I was already at such a low point, I didn't really know where to go from there. So seeking the help of a pastor and psychologist was my next step to improve my life. With their help, I was able to start accepting that I could change and that I could improve myself that I wouldn't always be where I was currently at.

I think for a lot of people, there has to be something to push you to start to make the changes you want to make. There has to be something there that forces you to look at your life and identify that there are problems you need to work through. There has to be something there that shows you that life could be better and that you can make it better. For me, the catalyst for change was pain. I was in so much pain and while I thought about other ways to escape it, I knew that simply put, I just didn't want to hurt anymore. And since I wasn't ready to leave this world, I had to find another way to make the pain stop.

So many people turn to harmful ways to help them cope with their pain. All we want is to escape and the easiest ways to do that is to, in some way, distance ourselves from reality. Some people do this through drugs, alcohol, self-harm, or suicide. For me, it was thoughts of suicide that were my idea of escape. Being depressed hurt me and after looking at my life, I realized I had to take a step that wasn't self-harming. I had to take that first step.

Did you know that action can cure a lot of things? And inaction can cause more harm than good. For me, the action of actually pulling into the church's parking lot started the process. The action of thinking about my dog started the process. The action of accepting that I wanted to get better, made me call the psychologist. Action can do a lot of good, so long as that action isn't just running away, or staying where you're at.

So what action will you take?

Think about the vision that you have for yourself and for your life. What do you want? Write it down, and once you have it, reverse engineer it and take that first step.

Reverse engineering means you look at your goal or how you want your life to be, and you look at all the things that will get you there. Think about it like building a skill on how to cook gravy. Your ultimate goal is to cook good gravy. So, do you just throw the ingredients in a pan and hope for the best? No. You look at all the steps you need to do. You'll have a lot of steps in between first watching a YouTube video about making gravy to actually making good gravy. You have to figure out each step. Watching the video will only show you what you have to do, but it's only through experience that you'll learn. Where do you start? Maybe by getting a pan. Which pan? And then putting it on a stove burner. How do you turn that on? Then put the heat to the bottom of the pan. How hot should it be? How hot will it get? And so on. Each little step is part of the whole. They all build upon one another and the first time you make gravy, it will probably be okay, but not great, or really bad. So you keep practicing and you keep getting better until you reach your goal.

The gravy example is simple, but most goals in life aren't as simple. So what's your ultimate goal, and what are the steps you want to take to reach it? I learned from an amazing friend in Utah that if you want to get to where you want to go, you have to reverse engineer how to get there. Once you know the steps, take each small one to reach your goal. Even if you only take one tiny step, hey, you've done it. You've taken a step. You've taken some action. You've progressed in some way. Don't do an all-out sprint to your goal since that will probably just wear you out and get you nowhere. Take your small steps. Don't just think about it. Do it. Delaying action helps no one, especially not you.

You are worth making a change for a better life. You deserve it. So go for it and take your one step. Then take the next.

Connecting Lessons with Food

Delicious Salmon- pan fried

Ingredients

- Salmon- individual portion or fillet
- 1-2 Tbsp. cooking oil of choice
- Kosher salt - varies according to portion size (apply lightly)

Warm pan to medium heat and add oil as pan is warming up.

Salt the skin side of portion

Place skin side down first, turn as the center gets lighter color and partially cover. Best if you have glass lids to see while cooking

You will see the color change to a lighter color and can turn a bit beige or cream color. Salmon is actually done before it looks done

Cook to an internal temperature of 145 degrees, remove from heat and let rest for a minimum of 3-4 minutes before serving.

Lemon slices can be added while cooking if desired.

Lemon juice can also be added for a bit of extra flavor.

Salmon goes great with a fresh side salad, warm bread and your favorite vegetables.

Chapter Three

Learn a New Hobby

I can honestly say I learned a lot from my psychologist. He helped me start to pull myself out of my depressed state. He helped me also identify patterns that just weren't serving me well anymore. I went to work, had a tough time, came home, played with my dog, ate dinner, and went to bed. This pattern, while okay, wasn't really helping me at all. It gave me a lot of time to keep thinking about my problems over and over, giving me the chance to sink deeper into depression. So while I could keep up with doing nothing at home, it was probably better to find something else. He recommended that I take up a hobby to help keep my brain busy, and to give me something interesting to come home to, besides my dog.

But what was I supposed to do as a hobby? You might think that I immediately gravitated to cooking, but I actually turned to something else instead. Growing up on a ranch, I learned how to work with my hands to get things done. I learned how to use tools and random pieces of material to make new things or to at least make things work again.

My dad wasn't the type of guy to pay for a man to fix something for him. Instead, we would have to make do, or fix it ourselves. When I went back to Montana after the military, I learned quickly to use tools to MacGyver repairs out of a bit of wire and whatever other scraps were laying around, and honestly, some things just couldn't be fixed. I think the ranch must have lost hundreds of thousands of dollars over the years because things weren't repaired the way they needed to be. So I eventually learned how to repair things as part of that work and later work in different situations. Tools were things I knew how to use and were things that I was comfortable around.

When I was asked to find a hobby to help me get healthier, I naturally gravitated to tools and using them to build or rebuild things. So I decided to build a little shop in my garage. I set up the tools I would need to create or fix things. It seemed really fitting that as I was trying to rebuild my life, I could also physically build things to make me a little happier. I went into my shop one day and built some benches. They were really simple, but they were things I made with my own two hands. I painted them and made them look nice. That was my first step in a new hobby. As I continued trying out this hobby, I mostly stuck with simple things. At that time, I didn't really have the confidence to try to build bigger items. I also didn't venture too far into repairing mechanical things or other items. I stuck with the things I felt confident about. I was still in that fixed mindset but I was working on it.

I gathered a lot of materials in my shop to give me the most options of things I could try and build, but I honestly didn't finish a lot of projects. I was still in that mindset that everything had to be perfect if I worked on it, even if it was completely new to me. So I would end up getting frustrated by my projects. It was hard and if things didn't go my way, I just tossed the project aside and moved on to something else. You can see here that even though I had picked up a new hobby, I was repeating a lot of my familiar patterns. If things were difficult, I simply tossed them aside and moved on to something else, not learning from my mistakes and not trying to problem solve. I just moved on. Eventually, I got to the point where I was completely done with the experience. I just figured that I sucked at this hobby like I did at a lot of other things. It wasn't for me so I was done. I threw out all of the materials I collected and all of the unfinished projects. The only things I kept were my tools.

At some point, I met up with a very trusted friend of mine who was really good at building things. He was the most talented guy I knew and he could just make the most beautiful things, a real craftsman. When we were hanging out, we got to talking about the hobby that I had thrown away. He explained that nobody is perfect in a new hobby at first. Even he, someone who was arguably a master at his craft, made frequent mistakes or screwed up a whole project. But did that mean that he just threw the project away and did something he was familiar with? No! He told me that, he might throw away that project, but he started the exact same project over again, learning from his mistakes and using his experience to make it better the next time around. It's completely normal not to have everything turn out okay the first time you do it. Instead, learn from the failure or mistake and try it again. Try to get better instead of moving onto something else entirely different.

His words really inspired me to try again. So once more, I gathered some materials and started building things again. I even started to branch out into new directions. And yeah, I made a lot of mistakes. While they still brought me low, I was able to try and learn from the mistakes. I slowly started getting better and eventually, my confidence started to grow. I continued with this hobby for quite a long time, using it as a way to keep my mind busy and improve my mental health.

Eventually, I moved back to our ranch in Montana just before my dad passed, and I ended up putting my hobbies on hold to focus on the ranch instead. Ranching and farming is crazy hard work and just keeping it above water was exhausting. I spent hours each day focused on farming work and trying to keep the whole thing going. With my hobbies set aside, I didn't really have another means to escape the stress and exhaustion brought on by the work. As winter rolled around, I found myself slipping back into old habits and becoming more and more depressed once again. The winters are long and once I became aware of my slow slink back into depression, I wanted to stop it before it got a hold of me again. I realized I needed a hobby more than ever before to help me get through the winters in Montana and to help me return to a better mental state. So I started the hunt for a new hobby, something that would really inspire me and keep me engaged for a long time.

One day, I was just flipping through the TV channels and I ended up watching this show where some guys go and find old cars. I mean really run-down cars that won't run again. These guys go and they pick up the cars and fix them up. They would rebuild the car to match it's old-style or turn it into something new. They picked up a piece of junk that was otherwise just rusting away, and turned it into something useful again. After watching the show for a while, I realized that was something I would like to try too. Finding something that seems like it's worthless and turning it into something beautiful and worthy is another pretty good analogy for my life.

Having had some experience building boats in Florida, I had the mechanical know-how on how to work with vehicles, though I still had a lot to learn about the whole process. But having a passion for learning how to build up and repair cars wasn't something that came to me out of the blue. Sure, that TV show really did trigger me and cause me to want to try refurbishing vehicles, but I had loved cars since I was a younger kid.

After my parents were divorced, my mom and I lived alone and I eventually learned how to drive. While I was in high school, I bought this really beautiful pickup truck. It was one of the best vehicles I ever owned and I loved that truck. It was precious to me, but it was also a symbol and means of my escape whenever things weren't going well at home. I would often just jump into my pickup and drive away, going wherever I wanted to escape the situation. That pickup was like my friend. It always brought me to safer places and carried me wherever I wanted to go, anytime I wanted to go there. Because I loved this pickup so much, I took really good care of it. I maintained it, always cleaned it, and made sure that it was running like a dream. I later sold the truck and it was one of my biggest regrets, but years later, I ended up finding it again. The exact same pickup. I bought it back, fixed her up nice again, and it was one of the best vehicles I've ever owned.

Because I had this love for cars from back when I was a teenager, and because this TV show had inspired me to learn more about building up and refurbishing cars, I decided to go ahead and take a leap. I wanted to try it as a new hobby. So, just like with my previous hobby, I dived right into it. I gathered a lot of materials, and parts for cars and I started working on different vehicles. Like with my first hobby, it was a learning process, and I made a lot of mistakes. But the difference was that at this point, I was learning that mistakes were okay, so long as I learned from them and made improvements.

Building up cars really brought a lot of joy into my life. It was nice being able to solve a problem and figure out why a car wouldn't run or why I couldn't get it to work the way I wanted it to. Being able to find parts online, really anything I wanted, and having it be delivered right to my door, also made it a lot easier than if I had to search by hand for parts in junkyards. I loved how I could take a piece of junk and turn it into a car that was once again useful. I would often bring them to community car shows or races as a means of meeting people. So this hobby not only brought me the joy of successfully problem-solving, but also connected me with the community in a deeper way. Bringing cars to car shows means that you get to connect with other car enthusiasts. It meant that I built more friendships and learned more from the people in my community.

In the end, both hobbies of mine took my mind off the pain of the suffering I experienced. They gave me a new purpose when I was feeling purposeless. It didn't matter whether I had a lot of work, or a lot of things I needed to accomplish, hobbies are what gave me a sense of fulfillment. They helped me create new patterns of living, but also develop my mindset so that I could improve my self-perceptions. As I improved my skills, I started to feel better about myself and was more able to convince myself that I wasn't a screwup. I was able to actually finish things and feel that sense of satisfaction that I was good at something in my life. My hobbies helped to influence the story of myself and gave me a better perception of what I was capable of doing.

Benefits of Hobbies

I think that when we talk about hobbies, our culture tends to think that they're frivolous things. After all, a hobby probably isn't going to bring in any money, and I think that for a lot of people, that makes hobbies seem useless. But hobbies aren't distractions from life, and whether you believe it or not, most people have time for a hobby in their life. I can't really express just how much my hobbies helped me, but I do want to talk about the benefits of hobbies that I noticed. I think that anyone could benefit from picking up a hobby, especially if you're struggling with your self-perception. Doing a hobby that is low stakes, like cooking for fun, building little things, or even rebuilding cars can be a great way to improve your opinion of yourself and improve your self-love. So here are some of the benefits I think hobbies provide us.

Hobbies help us cope with rough times. Whenever we're having a tough day, month, year, our minds can become just stuck on the problem. We may not be in the position to solve the problem, but our minds will focus so much on it that it becomes the center of our present existence. Hobbies help separate us from the things stressing us out. For me, my hobbies helped me cope with terrible work situations or living situations. They gave me a break from the mundane, day to day struggle of making a living. So all of a sudden, instead of focusing on how horrible I felt my life was, I instead got to focus on something that engaged me in a different way, and eventually, it would take my mind off stressful or depressing events and help me focus on the present moment.

Going off the idea of the present moment, hobbies are often strongly connected with mindfulness, or actively focusing on the present moment instead of the past or future. By focusing on the present moment, we can set aside our stress and instead just focus on what is happening right now. With a very physical hobby like building, you always have to be mentally present to avoid accidents or harm. That focus on the present really calms the mind. By concentrating on what's directly in front of me, I'm able to distance myself from previous anxiety or sadness and instead pay attention to what my hands are doing and what I'm creating right in the here and now. That moment of rejuvenation really helps to settle my mind and gives me a sense of peace by the end of the day.

They also provide us with richness in our life. Before I picked up a hobby back when I was seriously depressed, I didn't do much with my life beyond working or hanging out with my dog. My days ran together and there was no additional oomph to my life. Adding a hobby to the mix helped me create a more interesting life. All of a sudden, I had something to do once I got home. But more than that, having the hobby helped me round out my own development. It taught me new skills, and developed skills I didn't even recognize as having. When I was refurbishing cars, I also gained a new piece to my life. All of a sudden, I got to interact with more people than I normally would have. I talked to people online in the search for parts, and once I finished a car, bringing it to a car show also brought me to new people.

Getting those connections helped to enrich my life but also having people look at the work I had done gave me a sense of even greater accomplishment. I did that. My hard work did that. My life turned from something dull and gray into something full of color just by including a new experience in it. I think the community aspect of hobbies really sealed the deal for me, since it opened my world to meeting people with similar interests to mine.

Hobbies can inspire you. If you've ever just felt run down by life, you know what I mean about missing inspiration in your life. Your days just run together, and maybe you don't feel passionate about things anymore. A new hobby can restart your passion. Having something you are genuinely excited about can help you not only improve your hobby skills but also improve your creativity and problem-solving skills. Hobbies teach us lessons that we may not otherwise learn, and they can provide a lot of creative inspiration for our day by day activities.

Finally, hobbies give us a new target to reach, and a new goal to have. Having a goal can really provide you with a fulfilling life. Your goals don't have to be career-based; they just have to be there. So for me, my hobbies provided me with some purpose. I had goals to get better or to build up this car or find this part. When I succeeded with those goals, I felt amazing. Successfully achieving goals and then creating new ones gives me a sense of purpose. And while I may not get that same sense in other places, I'll definitely be able to get that from my hobbies.

So I believe that hobbies are incredibly beneficial to everyone. I'm genuinely happy my psychologist recommended that I pick up a hobby and I really encourage you to also pick one up.

Finding a New or Old Hobby

Because finding hobbies can be so helpful to us, like it was for me, I really think that everyone should take the time to really identify hobbies they want to try. For me, I ended up choosing hobbies that were from my past. I used previous passions or skills to help me create a hobby that I truly enjoyed. I think that when we're going through a hard time in life, we can look back and find things that brought us joy and use those things in the present to bring us joy again. That's where we can find our hobbies. For me, this meant that I remembered my passion for my pickup truck, and brought that same passion back years later to create a hobby I genuinely enjoyed. When I picked up cooking as a new hobby, I looked back and remembered learning to cook from my mom and grandmothers. Bringing that forward into my present life brought with it the fondness of memories and the passion for new experiences.

If you want to find a new hobby for yourself, then you could also look back in your past to find things that you're passionate about. As children we all have things we're interested in, things that make our hearts race and our eyes open with wonder. For me, that was cars, helicopters, cooking, and so much more. Every child is passionate about something in their life, whether it's something that is actively around them, or a dream they have for the future. You also had dreams like this, so reflect on them. Look back at your past and find the things you were crazy about and if you can't remember, maybe reach out to some family members who might remember for you. I guarantee you that there were at least some things you were excited about that you could try to get into as an adult, even if it seems impractical.

Maybe you wanted to be a racecar driver or a doctor. Maybe you wanted to travel around the world, or play awesome music. Whatever your passion might have been, reflect on it. What about it made it so interesting to you? Why was it so inspiring? And is it still inspiring? If the answer is yes to that last question, then find a way to incorporate that inspiration into your life as an adult. If you loved dogs as a kid and wanted to be a vet, but you're now a business person, incorporate something with animals in your life today. Find a hobby like volunteering at an animal shelter, fostering pets, training pets, whatever really interests you. Find ways to take a childhood passion and turn it into a hobby for your life now.

My childhood dream was to become a helicopter pilot. It was all because of a show I watched on TV, but I remember being six and just being so fascinated by helicopters. Watching them move across the sky was just amazing for me. And I knew in that moment that that was what I wanted. I wanted to be a helicopter pilot more than anything else in my life. I wanted to fly helicopters just as skillfully as those pilots in that show did. So when I joined the army as an adult, you can imagine just how excited I was about the possibility of flying in and eventually piloting a helicopter. It was like a dream come true being around them and trying to get approved for pilot training. I was close to having my dream come true too. And one day, I did get to fly in a helicopter, but it wasn't in the way I was hoping for.

I was on a training mission in the army and it was absolutely pitch black that night. My convoy was traveling in a vehicle with an open-top, with our lights off, trying to navigate an area. There was a low hanging tree branch that I didn't see and it slammed right into me. That tree branch struck me so hard that I broke and damaged a large portion of my face, especially my eye. That night I got to fly in a helicopter as it took me from the field to a local hospital. And let me tell you that was a bummer.

My injury was so severe that I stayed in the hospital for a long time, trying to have my eye socket reconstructed. I spent a year and a half in the hospital and went through about five surgeries to repair my face. And while it was great to have the damage repaired, it meant the end of the dream of flying a helicopter. I was no longer qualified to fly one in the army, and my limited sight in that eye meant that flying outside of the army wasn't in my cards either.

Knowing that my ultimate dream at the time was over made me feel quite sorry for myself. I mean, I was so close to achieving that dream, and all of a sudden it was taken away from me in a permanent way. It definitely didn't help that at this time, I was still living with my negative self-perception and I used the injury to really beat myself up. But one day at the hospital I ran across this other recruit, a kid really, who was about 18 years old. We ended up chatting about our stays and he told me his story. After joining basic training, and just a couple of months into his time in the army, he started having some serious foot pain. Turned out, he had cancer in his foot.

While the doctors tried to stop the cancer, they weren't really successful, and in the end, they amputated his foot in an attempt to keep cancer from spreading. However, that also wasn't successful. They kept trying to stop cancer. Eventually, they removed his whole leg at the hip and successfully stopped the spread of cancer. So while I was crying over the loss of a dream, this kid just lost a huge part of his body, something that would end his career and change his life.

That day was really an eye-opener for me. Here was this happy-go-lucky kid who wouldn't let his missing leg stop him or keep him from his dreams, and here was me, crying because I couldn't fly a helicopter. So that discussion really helped me keep my life in perspective. I had to make a new dream and pick up other things. Since I couldn't fly a helicopter, I started spending more time riding in them because I still enjoyed helicopters, I just had to enjoy them in a different way. I can't do that as much now because of age and also developing eye problems, but I was able to do some parts of my childhood dream and turn it into fun experiences that really benefited me.

So, if you look back at your own childhood, or maybe missed dreams, what are some things you could bring into your life now? And if you can't think of anything from childhood, then find hobbies in other areas. Look on social media, check-in with your friends, and find things that you think will be fun.

For me, losing the chance to work with and around helicopters was sad, but it led me to appreciate other mechanical things and eventually led to me enjoying my hobby of fixing up cars. It doesn't matter if your dreams have changed from childhood. After all, that's to be somewhat expected. Only a couple of us are truly lucky enough to have turned our childhood dreams into active careers. So take your dreams and turn them into hobbies. The point I'm trying to make is to pick up a hobby, any hobby. It will add so much value to your life and also to your self-perception.

Connecting Lessons with Food

Honey Infused Corn Bread

Ingredients:

- 1 cup all-purpose flour
- 1 cup yellow corn meal
- ¼ cup vegetable oil
- ¼ cup white sugar
- 1 Tbsp. baking powder
- ½ tsp. salt
- 2 eggs beaten
- 1/3 cup fresh honey
- 1 cup whipping cream
- Non-stick spray or butter

Combine the flour, sugar, cornmeal, salt and baking powder and mix.

In another bowl mix the beaten eggs with the cream, honey and oil and beat well together.

Stir in the dry ingredients so they are just moistened.

In a 9" square baking pan or dish, grease the sides and bottom.

Pour mixture into a baking dish and bake uncovered at 400 degrees for 20-25 minutes and check with a wooden toothpick and make sure the toothpick comes out clean. Sometimes the center will rise quite high in the pan so make sure that part is fully cooked.

This is so good with real butter. I love the Kerrygold brand. Amazing!

Chapter Four

Identify Your Bliss

This topic is so close to the previous one about hobbies, but when I say identify your bliss, I really mean find things that make you happy and go for them. Throughout our lives, we are influenced by the people around us, including our parents and these people all have expectations for us. These expectations can influence what we do with ourselves or with our lives. There are so many people out there who have a job or career or a life that was dictated by their parent's expectations rather than from making them genuinely happy. This nearly happened for me, as my dad wanted me to be a rancher my whole life. And if I had stayed in his home, I might have been. But I decided to try other things in my life.

Sure, some of it was running away from other problems, but overall, it led me to things that made me happy.

So find the things that make you happy in your life and go for it. Don't just follow what other people are doing and instead go for the things that make you particularly happy. On social media or even just blogs and such, you'll read stories about the amazing things people are doing in their life. For a lot of us, we want to do the exact same thing in an attempt to be happy, but the only person who can make you happy is you. And the only person who knows what will make you happy is you. So we all have to take the time to genuinely find the things that will make us happy in life, instead of following the "mainstream" happiness route, since that might not work for your life.

When my time in the army came to an end, I wasn't really sure what to do or where to go. So I returned to the only place I really knew, Montana but I had already seen what was out there and I wasn't very satisfied with my life there. For the first time in my life, I decided to stop and really think about what I wanted with my life. I had a vague idea, but I knew that I was miserable in the winter in Montana, so I wanted to go somewhere warm.

I had enjoyed my time in Georgia and Florida when I was in the army and I thought I could be happy in a place with warm weather like that. So I made the choice to leave my life in Montana and go into the unknown in Florida. My father and I had a relationship that was strained and sometimes very poor. I told my dad that I was moving from Montana, but more than that, that I wouldn't be contacting him again. That was February 2nd, 1986.

I was able to reach out to a friend who also wanted a change in direction and together, we drove all the way from Montana to Florida. I didn't really have a clear idea of what I wanted to do in Florida, but I wanted to pursue things that were interesting to me. I've always loved boats, so this was my chance to dive into that interest. During the drive, I told my friend about a great bar I visited in Florida while I was in the army. It was called Bennigan's and it had the most amazing energy. The food and drinks there were awesome and I just thought it was the coolest place I had been. I figured, hey, I wouldn't mind working at a place like that as a bartender. So when I got to Florida, that's what I looked for.

I went to a bartending school and I actually ended up getting a job bartending at Bennigan's in Sarasota, Florida. It was an amazing dream come true when I thought most of my dreams were over. I was only 36 years old at that time. It was an accomplishment that I wasn't sure I could actually achieve, but I was so thrilled by my success. It was my first time pursuing a dream that I actually thought was attainable and even though I hoped for it, I couldn't believe that it actually came true.

Choosing to follow that path was something that greatly changed my life. It led to more opportunities than I would have ever had in Montana and gave me the chance to really find my bliss. It helped me find the things that made me happy, and while I was still struggling with self-worth, I felt lighter than I had in years.

During my time in Florida, I started to get interested in something else there. As I mentioned before, I had always found mechanical things interesting, from caring for my pickup to looking at helicopters. I had learned a lot through experience in and out of the army and so vehicles of all types were an interest to me. While I was working as a bartender in Florida, I got to meet some guys who did offshore racing in those large racing boats. Seeing them glide through the water and seeing how they worked was just so fascinating to me. I started to have a new goal of getting to work on those boats and work around the water. Those boats were amazing and beautiful and I loved their architecture.

I eventually got my chance. I met a lot of connections at the bar and they introduced me to the offshore racing teams. They helped me get involved in the whole thing and learned more about how the boats were built and maintained. I got the chance to work with several other boat builders and I really learned a lot. Getting that opportunity was amazing and I can never regret it. Building boats, watching them race was one of the highlights of my life. It was easily the best job I ever had and it was the best time of my life. The most amazing thing to me was that I made those choices on my own, after years of following what others wanted me to do.

Before moving to Florida, and really throughout my early life, I really wanted to meet my dad's expectations. Because of that want, I tried to seek his approval in things, especially before joining the army. But joining the military was the first chance I had to really separate myself emotionally from him. That distance helped me realize that I couldn't meet his expectations and that I had to make my own. After losing my chance of becoming a helicopter pilot, and after leaving the army, I returned to Montana, thinking that I would be okay with his expectations still. But I wasn't. When I took the step to leave my dad's influence and find the things that made me happy, I was able to finally meet my own expectations. Going to Florida was my choice and it led to my chance to find out who I was and what I wanted. I identified my bliss, or my bliss at the time anyways.

Find something you're really passionate about. There's something truly glorious about living every day doing something that you're excited about. Find that thing that keeps you up at night with excitement. Find something that you love so much that you want to do it for the rest of your life. Identify your bliss.

When you find that thing, that job or career that brings you such joy, it no longer becomes work. Heck, you might not even make money off of it, but it fulfills you in a way that other activities don't. That's the goal you want to head towards. That's the thing you'll want to do with your life. And if you do identify it but let it pass in order to meet the expectations of other people, you'll probably regret it.

If I hadn't left Montana to move to the south, I would have regretted it. I wouldn't have learned nearly as much as I did while being in the south. I wouldn't have had the chance to find happiness first bartending and then working on boats. Instead, I would have stayed in Montana living with daily pain and hurt until there was nothing of me left. I also would have regretted just not going for it. After all, it wasn't like getting into a car and driving to Florida was physically hard. That one step wasn't as challenging as, say, going for your pilot's license or going through basic training. So I would have regretted not taking that step, especially because it was one that was physically simple.

I think the hardest part of finding your bliss is actually going for it. Leaving Montana was hard in a way because of the unknown. I didn't know what life would be like in Florida, but I was hopeful. I figured that life was so miserable in

Montana, was I going to stick it out to avoid possible future pain in Florida? No. I decided that it might be easier to transition into the unknown and hope for the best. And for me, it worked out. The moment I got out of the car in Florida and felt the full warm sun on my skin I knew I had made the right decision. Driving onto the sand at Daytona beach made the whole adventure worth it. Leaving, for me, was worth it.

While making the change was the right choice for me, I know that for a lot of people, making large changes like that is incredibly hard, especially if the change is risky. If you've taken the time to determine what will make you happiest, the choice to actually pursue that thing can be fraught with anxiety. After all, you're making a change to go for something that you may not know will pan out and that can cause a lot of fear about the risk. However, I urge you to really consider this: If you chose to stay static, then that's fine but what have you missed out on by staying?

Don't let your fear of the unknown stop you from trying something new and exciting, whether it's a small change or a big one. We often fear risks simply because of this unknown. We don't know what's going to happen in the situation. Are we going to succeed or are we going to fail? That unknown can be so terrifying especially if we're already leaving a situation that's relatively safe.

A great example of this is someone who always wanted to join Broadway to sing. They have a choice, to leave a stable job and community and adventure into the unknown, where they'll have to audition and find housing, etc, without knowing the outcome. That's a huge change and they may find it to be risky but they have to weigh the risk. Stay at home and stay in your day to day job or take a risk. If they don't join Broadway or at least try, will they regret it? Only they can say whether they'll regret it or not.

Taking a risk like that is going to make anyone uncomfortable unless you're already uncomfortable and want a change. That's what happened to me. Because I was already experiencing negative things, I figured that since I was already at the bottom, things could only get better from there. It made the decision to leave easier than if I was leaving a great safety net. However, even if you're leaving a safety net, taking a risk can honestly be very rewarding. Sure, you're going to face obstacles and challenges, just like you would in any other new activity, but the results from that experience can help your overall personal growth. You'll start to be able to see what you're capable of doing.

Going to Florida taught me more than just how to bartend or how to care for and build boats. It taught me what I was capable of once I put my mind to it. It showed me that I could achieve my dreams and actually make something of my efforts. Going for your dreams can show you the same thing.

Whether your risk pans out or not, you'll learn a lot of great lessons from the venture. It will teach you what you're capable of and just how resilient you are. If you go for your bliss and take a chance on it, you'll quickly learn just how strong you are in tough situations. You'll learn how you handle yourself when faced with obstacles or when faced with success. You'll learn how creative you are and how to solve problems that come your way. And if you choose not to go for your dreams, you'll learn what it means to be steady and how to build a life with the cards you have in your deck. You may learn the same lessons about creativity and problem solving, but you may also not really get the chance to experiment and challenge yourself. In both situations, you're learning something, but how much you learn depends on just how much of a chance you're taking. Even if you choose to go after your bliss, and it fails, that's also okay. You'll have learned so much from the experience and you'll probably end up better for it. You'll walk away with new skills and concepts and be more prepared to face the unknown again in the future.

I highly recommend you go after the things that make you happy. I can't recommend it enough just because of how it affected my life and the lessons it taught me. But also because I've seen what happens when people choose to stay at home and not take the risk of leaving. If we choose not to pursue our bliss, we end up settling for what we can get. Maybe we stay in our hometown and miss out on all of the wonderful opportunities there are out there. Without risk, we end up settling for a life that doesn't have a lot of surprises or one where we feel like we're in control and safe. And if we settle into a situation that isn't safe, without taking risks, we won't have the skills to leave the situation without a big push.

In my area of Montana, if kids didn't leave the area to search for what they wanted in life, they ended up staying exactly where they were. They would marry young and have kids at a young age. And if their life wasn't safe or happy, like mine wasn't in Montana, they'll find ways to escape, even if they can't escape physically. A lot of people I knew growing up turned to drugs and alcohol to escape the lives they had settled into, not knowing that there were other options out there.

So take the chance. Find what makes you happy and go for it, even if there's some risk to that change. You'd be surprised what you can do or get by just making a change and going for what you want, instead of what other people want for you.

Connecting Lessons with Food

Baked Beans with Venison

Ingredients:

- 1 lb. ground venison, elk, moose etc.
- 1-15 oz. can red kidney beans (I drain and rinse)
- 1- 15 oz. can of pork and beans, I love the Bush's brand
- 1 pound of peppered bacon chopped up
- ½ of a yellow onion chopped
- ½ cup brown sugar
- ½ cup regular sugar
- 2 tbsp. apple cider vinegar
- 2 tbsp. mustard, use your favorite
- ½ cup of ketchup

In a Dutch oven, cook the bacon until almost done, (I do not drain the bacon), remove, then cook the burger until browned.

Return all the meat to the Dutch oven and add all of the beans first. Then add the rest of ingredients and make sure to stir as you add each.

Cook at 350 degrees for a minimum of 1 hour. To help retain moisture you can cover while cooking.

64

Serve with fresh baked bread, rolls and butter. French or Sourdough goes very well also. This goes fast so you may want to double the recipe. I love bacon but if you are not that much of a fan go with ½ of what is called for. But I bet you won't...

Chapter Five

Create Your Goals

I think the last several chapters have led us to this point, the ultimate importance of having goals in your life. Without goals, we end up wandering around just trying to make ends meet without really having something that supports us and fulfills us. Our goals in life don't have to be ones that are focused solely on our careers, but having goals, really any goals can help give our lives direction and help us make the most out of it. Small or large, goals are so critically important to everything we do.

See the Target, Hit the Target

One thing I learned from a friend of mine is how important it is to have a target, your goal, to clearly see it, and to get to it. If you don't have a target in mind, then how do you know if you've reached where you want to go? You can't hit what you don't know you're aiming at.

We can have general goals, but if we don't specify them then how can we know if we've made it to them?

I feel like most of my younger adult life I didn't have a specific target. I made choices as a way to escape things that I was struggling with and I often escaped without a goal in mind. My first escape, joining the military, helped me get out of Montana and the risk of unemployment. When I left the army, I was leaving behind some of my dreams about being a helicopter pilot, but I didn't really know what to do next. So I was kind of adrift, and when we're adrift, we tend to look for a safe place to land.

For the first time, I had some clear targets that I wanted to aim for. I wanted to be a bartender. So I took that goal, broke it into its smaller pieces, and finally accomplished what I wanted to do. My next target was to work on boats. So again, I took that target, broke it down into smaller ones, and got myself there. Setting these goals and having a clear direction to go into changed my life, but they were also the first time that I actually aimed for a specific goal. With clear things in mind, I was able to take steps to get there.

Another goal I can think of that I had was getting mentally well, and that only occurred after hitting rock bottom,

67

years after Florida. Again with this goal, I had to find the small pieces, the smaller goals to hit to bring me to my larger target. It took a long time, but then again, most large goals do take time.

Targets for our lives are so important, and I don't just mean the big targets like your five-year goal. I mean all targets. Having something to move towards can give our lives a positive direction that can help us feel like we're growing into something, instead of just floating along. Sometimes, and in some periods of our life, we don't have a target and if we don't have one, we won't know where to go. Without a target, our life can often seem like it's missing something maybe because it is: it's missing a direction.

After being in Florida for a while, I was without a clear target in mind, so I ended up floating along. One negative event led to another which led to another and so on until I felt like my life was just one terrible thing after another. Of course, a large portion of that had to do with my own mental health.

Depression can very easily change your perception of how your life is actually going. Being without a goal helped depression take root in my life and made it so hard to start a new goal. While I was eventually able to create new goals, it still took a long time to get to that point, and I needed a support system to get there.

The goals in our life will always change as we meet our them or as our life changes. We have to adapt our goals to fit with what is happening. As you reach for and accomplish targets, you'll start to make new ones. I had to make new targets. Eventually, I picked up and dropped hobbies, and each time I made a target and adapted it to the changes and challenges life threw at me. My current goal is to be the best cook I can be. But I also have other targets that are maybe larger, like wanting to be on the Beat Bobby Flay show. On that show, Bobby Flay brings on chefs and they try to cook and compete against him.

That's a goal that would be amazing for me to accomplish. I also want to meet Gordon Ramsay in the future. Having goals like these gives me something to work towards, but it's the other more community-focused goals that give my life a lot of purpose. One of my ongoing goals is to share my passion for food in my community. I want to share food with people and watch as they sit down and eat the meal I made. I want my food to make people happy and be memorable so they don't forget the great meal they shared with friends. Goals like this give me a clear direction of where I want to go with my skills and my life.

Having goals is amazing, but as we progress towards our goals, we have to keep in mind that they may not get accomplished, and that's ok. It's okay to not meet a goal or for a goal to fail. What matters is that you tried your best to get there and that you learn from the failure, as I mentioned before. This fear of failure was a hindrance to me in a lot of my life. If I failed at something, I often felt worthless, and I think this is a common feeling for a lot of people struggling with self-esteem and self-love. My expectations for myself can be brutal, especially since I didn't have a lot of self-confidence. But you know what? It's okay to fail because we're not always going to hit our targets. We learn from failure and we can make new targets.

One thing that helped me create good targets was really setting smaller goals, often through reverse engineering as I mentioned earlier. By having smaller targets, I was able to start reaching and accomplishing small goals. It helped build up my self-confidence and give me a chance to be successful at something when I felt like I couldn't be successful. If you want to go for goals, I recommend you do something similar. Start with smaller goals, or break your larger goals into something more manageable. That way, when you make a smaller accomplishment, you can be thrilled and even more passionately driven towards the larger goal.

Write Your Goals

When you start to consider the goals you have for your current moment, write them down. The worst thing that you can do is have a goal in your head and then forget it a couple of days later. Writing down your goals makes them concrete and makes them real to you. It turns an abstract idea into something you can look at and read and aim for. Having clear targets, after all, is the only way you're going to actually accomplish something. So write down your goals. You might write them in a journal or an app, but you can also write them on a piece of paper and place them somewhere you'll see them often. Seeing your goals daily can help remind you what you're working towards, and help you maintain some motivation to reach them.

What are your goals? How would you break them down into smaller pieces? Why are these your goal? These are three important questions to ask yourself. These answers can be the first thing you write down wherever you keep your goals list. This way, every time you see your goals, you're reminded of why you're pursuing them. This can be even more helpful if you struggle in general with setting your goals and maintaining your motivation to achieve them. Don't just leave these questions unanswered. These questions are the basis of your life at this moment.

They're your drive right now and these answers can give you the motivation to continue towards your goals, even after making a mistake or experiencing a failure. Once you've analyzed your motivations, it's time to look at your goals overall. Is your goal to save up for something, to retire early, follow your dream of singing on Broadway, to make the perfect gravy? Knowing your overall goal can help you then determine the steps you need to take to reach that goal. Having your goal broken down into smaller chunks can make them far more achievable.

One way of creating your goals is to create SMART goals. SMART is an acronym for the things that your goals should clearly spell out.

SMART goals are: Specific, Measurable, Attainable, Realistic, and Time-bound.

Specific goals are clearly spelled out and include all the information necessary to achieve the goal. They tell you when you'll know that the goal has been achieved. A goal, for example, might be, "I want to have extra money to complete my hobby of doll making". Or it can be something like, "I want to purchase a car". These goals are great, but they're not very specific. Instead of just stating the goal, consider all the aspects of that goal. Who is going to help you with your goal, how much money do you need, how will you know you've achieved your goal? These are all some questions you can consider when making your specific goal. So to remake the first goal as an example you might write: "I want to save $20 from each paycheck so that I can put it towards buying doll-making materials, which I will purchase in three months." This goal is very specific. It looks at more than just a general idea and gives you a clearly defined action to take. Once you have a specific goal in mind, then you need to determine how you'll know the goal has been achieved.

Measurable goals are easily evaluated. This means that they're goals where the final point is clearly marked. You know you've accomplished the goal because you've ended with a very clear result. It's proof that your goal has been met. If your goal is to save money, then you might say that seeing money in your bank account shows that you've met your goal, but this is really vague. Instead, you can have a specific amount in mind that you would like to see in the account, or you might say how much you're saving from each paycheck. A clear number or something tangible can be a very good indicator that your goal has been met. So if my goal was to be a helicopter pilot, then I would have used my pilot's license as an indicator that I've met my goal. That is a measurable, tangible result. If your goal has something that is measurable or something that can be recorded, then you'll know when you've absolutely accomplished your goal.

The next letter in the acronym is having an attainable goal.

Attainable goals are ones that are actually reachable. This means that they're something you can actually do in the amount of time you have or based on how much effort or hard work you can put into it. It also depends on the resources available to you. So if my goal is to be able to make the perfect gravy, I'll need to have the resources available to make that, like access to a stove, a recipe, and groceries. Without that access, this goal isn't attainable or it might be attainable but through a lot more difficulty than might be manageable. An attainable goal is one that fits into what you are actually capable of accomplishing. If your goal is beyond your current means or far beyond your current lifestyle or skills, then you'll need to find another goal or at least break it down a little more into chunks that are attainable.

Realistic goals are similar to attainable goals in that, they're things that you could realistically accomplish. So, I wanted to be a helicopter pilot, but with my eye injury, it's no longer a realistic goal since I'm not qualified to fly a helicopter without having good vision. So a realistic goal is one that you could reasonably accomplish with what you have available to you. Realistic goals have to also be relevant to you, and often the word realistic is replaced with the word relevant in the SMART goals acronym. A relevant goal is one that fits your life, and not someone else's. It's something that's important to you, not necessarily important to others. Realistic, relevant goals are ones that you can reasonably reach, not ones that are sky-high. If your goal is to earn a million dollars through day trading in a year, that's not really realistic, especially if you've never worked with trades before in your life. So choose goals that you can achieve. Otherwise, you'll end up disappointed in the results.

Finally, goals that are time-bound have clear cut deadlines so that you know when you'll accomplish them. Now, I admit that some of my goals aren't time-bound, but I think that having this really helps make your goals clear and gives you the necessary drive to go for it. Without a deadline on goals, it's easy to put them off until another time. It's like having that list of household chores you have to do. Without a clear deadline for having the chores completed, it's easy to just put them off. And then all of a sudden, it's been a year and your chore list is beyond a manageable level. So it's important to have deadlines set so that you will feel the drive to meet the goal by the deadline. If one of your goals is to lose weight and exercise, then having this goal end at a specific time will help keep you motivated to actually get there. How you chose to keep track of your deadlines and measure your times depends entirely on your organizational system, but also on the goal you have. You could write your goals and their timelines on a graph or in a bullet journal. You could use an app, or even put it on a large piece of paper in your kitchen. Having something that's very visually present in your life can help you feel some accomplishment as you start to meet your goals. Whichever way you choose to record your time-bound goals, having them to begin with will make your goals easier to achieve.

Once you've created your amazing goals, and have defined them using the SMART acronym, you'll be set up to actually work towards them. And hey, if the goal doesn't work out, that's okay. Take the time to reevaluate it. What happened? Why wasn't it achievable? How can you adapt it or completely change it? Consider these questions when remaking your goals. And if your goals are achieved, take some time to celebrate them and celebrate what you learned on the journey to accomplishing them. Pat yourself on the back and then set your next targets.

Connecting Lessons with Food

Creamy cracker spread

Ingredients:

- 1- 8 oz. pkg cream cheese
- 1- 5 oz. container Blue cheese crumbles (or use fresh if available)
- 3-4 oz. of chipped beef – chopped up
- Splash of Frank's hot sauce

Bring cream cheese to near room temperature for easy mixing

In a large mixing bowl mix the first 3 ingredients well. Add Frank's sauce to taste. Go easy at first it is very easy to overpower this recipe with the hot sauce.

Chill for at least 1 hour if possible, this helps bring the flavors together.

Serve with hors d'oeuvre. This is very good on Ritz crackers! But try a variety of crackers or small pieces of warm bread.

Small pieces of warm French bread are excellent!

Chapter Six

Create Good Habits

Read Books

As you start to take the time to change your life for the better, reading books can provide you with the motivation and support you need to either get started or to keep going. Books are one of the best ways that I keep myself motivated. I feel like I can learn so much from the wisdom of others, that I can genuinely change my life by using a book's advice. Whether that book is religious like the Bible or motivational like the ones written by great entrepreneurs, you can learn a lot from a good book.

I cannot overstate just how valuable books are for improving yourself. I never went to college, but I have always used books to make sense of the world around me and to learn and grow. It doesn't matter what your walk of life is, so long as you can read, you're set to succeed. You just have to open the right book. There is a wealth of wisdom out there and it's so easily accessible. Even your local library will have some amazing books you can use to turn your life around.

Books can influence you far more than watching a TV show ever could. Think about it this way; when you watch TV, you are a passive observer. You see what happens, but you don't experience anything or create anything. You don't even have to mentally digest anything, as evidenced by anyone who's ever zoned out while watching TV. But books on the other hand require your active participation. You have to be engaged. You have to turn the page. You have to digest what you've read. Otherwise, you would just close the book and turn on the TV for your nightly entertainment. Books can engage you more than other forms of entertainment, while also educating you about the ideas of others and the world around you.

What's amazing about reading a book, is that it often doesn't matter what kind of book it is, you can still learn a lot. Whether the book you're reading is fiction or non-fiction doesn't seem to matter. You can still learn a lot from it and learn to expand your own thinking. When it comes to creating goals and targets, you can often learn how to reach those targets by reading books by others who have already gotten there.

I love to read and I do it almost daily. And as I read, I write what I've learned and what I'm analyzing in the margins of the book. It helps me keep my notes right there and present while I digest what I've learned. It's my way of keeping up to date with ideas from others, but also my way of changing how I view myself and the world around me. Reading gives me multiple perspectives that I can pull from and use to influence my own ideas and goals.

If you're someone who is really busy or feels like you don't have the time to sit down and read, I want to challenge you to find a couple of minutes during the day to read. Reading doesn't take up much time, and all you have to do is take a short break from social media to read for about 10 minutes before continuing on with your day. In that short time, you'll have learned something, whether it's something new or old. And who knows, given 10 minutes, maybe you'll read something interesting enough that you keep right on reading. You may find new inspiration that way. And if you really are crazy busy, cut that time down to 5 minutes, but the point is to just read. Try it and see what you learn. I guarantee you'll learn more from reading a good book than you'll learn from reading your Facebook page or your Twitter feed.

If you want some recommendations for good books to read, start with the Bible, which is in my opinion one of the greatest books you can read to find peace and information on self-improvement. Another good book is Make Your Bed, by William H. McRaven. This book can teach you more about taking those first steps and having small, tiny goals to inspire you to move forward in your life. Ed Mylett's *#Max Out Your Life* is another great book to help inspire you to make changes in your life. It definitely inspired me to make changes in mine. The book Wild at Heart by John Eldredge is a book that was incredibly helpful to my life and taught me the value of taking risks. These four books alone are just a small portion of the books that I've read and an even smaller portion of the amazing books that are out there available to you for you to learn from.

Because there's just a wealth of knowledge out there in the pages of a good book, I strongly, so strongly urge you to start reading books. You can find books everywhere and anywhere but just take the time really stop and open one up. I guarantee you'll learn something new that you can then apply to your life.

Become Addicted to Saving Money

Saving money is one of those habits that everyone tells you to do but it's really hard. I remember reading once that most Americans are in serious debt, with very little if any savings. The truth is, my family and I were also a part of that statistic. Money for us was something that came in and very quickly went back out again. It was spent on important things but also spent on frivolous things. So naturally, when I started working on my own, I followed that advice to a tee. I spent money as I received it and didn't really have any savings. My spending habits got a lot worse when the depression hit me hard. I had to find a way to cope with the depression and spending money or doing some retail therapy, was a great way to make me feel better for a bit, right before I felt worse again. I would spend all of my money on expensive things that I often never ended up using. It was satisfying purchasing them, but ultimately a waste of my funds. Shopping only made me happier for a little blip of time, but that tiny amount of happiness was enough for me to maintain my poor money habits and keep money out of my hands. It wasn't until I was learning to manage depression and finding new habits that I started trying to learn how to save money. It was actually Ed Mylett who got me thinking about saving money.

Mylett mentioned that it's important to stop living above your means and instead become addicted to saving money. I hadn't really considered this before, but it kind of hit me hard. I needed to start living with what I have, buying what I could afford, and then saving more every day. His advice, and the words "become addicted to saving money" really influenced me and I tried to start doing so. But hearing some words and actually following through with them is really difficult.

Saving money wasn't in my experience or, it felt like it wasn't in my cards. I just couldn't manage to put money aside to save. So one day I signed up for Dave Ramsey's financial Peace University. It's a pretty amazing curriculum that shows you how to start saving money using some straightforward baby steps. Ramsey creates a big goal (saving money) and breaks it down into manageable chunks, reverse engineering the goals so that they are achievable. Ramsey's course has seven steps and the first one is to put a thousand dollars in your savings account. Now, a thousand dollars doesn't sound like a lot, but it does if you're someone who lives paycheck to paycheck like I did.

I eventually learned that there aren't a lot of people out there who have a thousand dollars stashed away for a rainy day. I wasn't the only one it was hard for. But I tried to follow Ramsey's steps and I slowly but surely started saving up a bit. I eventually hit that one-thousand-dollar mark and let me tell you that was quite an accomplishment for me. Not only had I reached a goal I had set, but having the money set aside and knowing that I wouldn't spend it frivolously was like a weight off my shoulder. I don't know how to really explain that feeling except as the best feeling ever.

Having that thousand dollars set aside meant that I was ready and prepared for anything to come my way. A thousand dollars was rent for a couple of months, or bills for a couple of months. It was a means to pay for my car if it broke down on the side of the road or to help a family member when they're in desperate need of money. It was a safety net that I didn't even realize I needed. Having that thousand dollars also meant that I wouldn't need to rely on a credit card to cover any emergency expenses. It set me up to succeed and to save more money in the future. Dave Ramsey sure knows what he's talking about when it comes to wise money usage.

I learned from that experience that having money in the bank means that you can do more of what you need to get done. Let me explain this a little. Instead of spending my money immediately on the next thing I absolutely "needed", having the money in the bank account meant that I could use it in the future for things that I actually had to get done. It meant that I could do more in my life since I had the money to support that, rather than having something new and materialistic that I might not even use. The more money you have set aside, the more things you can do with it. Saving money also made it very clear what I was missing out on because I didn't have money. If I didn't have money available, I missed out on opportunities like traveling or learning more from professionals, etc.

I used the words of two men who are financially wise to help set myself up for success with money. Ramsey's and Mylett's words helped me realize that I was the one who put myself in a position to be without money, and I was the one who could get myself out again. I could make sure that I had money to do what I wanted to do, while also having money set aside for emergencies I couldn't control or anticipate.

I urge you to also consider changing your financial habits so that you have some money saved. Keep my lessons in mind and remember to use the money on things that you absolutely want to get done, instead of on frivolous things you might never use. Become addicted to saving money by taking some small steps. Just like how we've discussed throughout this book, reverse engineer your goal. Start by putting aside five dollars from every paycheck. Then increase it to ten dollars every paycheck. You'll find that even if you save a little at a time, you'll still in the end have money set away. You'll eventually meet your savings goal, and once you get there, it will be like a weight off your shoulder. One day you'll have a rainy day and that money will come in handy.

Once I got into saving money, it became a little easier. I also found that I started to be hesitant to make big purchases unless I absolutely had to. I became a little more frugal and discerning with my purchasing choices. For example, one day I wanted to build a bigger shop for working on cars and I nearly took out a loan for it. But I decided to do the smart thing and not put myself into debt. Instead, I sold things I didn't need and sold some of the vehicles I had already repaired. It all worked out. So, I recommend you become addicted to saving money and make that change in your habits. That way, you'll always be prepared for a tough situation.

Connecting Lessons with Food

My favorite Stir Fry

Ingredients:

- 2- Chicken breasts
- 2- Pork boneless ribs
- ½ lb. peppered bacon
- 3 medium stalks of celery chopped
- 3 carrots chopped
- ½ yellow onion chopped
- ¼ cup shaved almonds
- 1.5 cups sliced mushrooms
- 2 tbsp. soy sauce or to taste
- 3 tbsp. +/- Olive oil

Cut all meat into bite size pieces.

Heat wok over medium high heat, add oil, then meat and cook until it looks done on the outside. Add soy sauce, then vegetables and cook until heated through.

There are so many things that can be served as a side with this recipe. Depending on your tastes and mood could be fresh cut raw vegetables, cheesy potatoes, mashed potatoes, stuffing- the list goes on..

RECIPES FOR A GREAT LIFE

Chapter Seven

Find Your Tribe

When you're trying to make a large change in your life, whether that's through pursuing large goals, taking new chances, or by trying to improve your own mindset, it's easier to make that change with the support of loving people. Without that support, everything becomes infinitely harder. So you want to have a support system in place, a tribe of friends and family members who have your back as you grow and develop yourself.

When I was depressed and without a goal in mind, I didn't have any friends outside of my very supportive cousin. I didn't have anyone else thought to turn to for help and a large part of that was because it's hard to make friends and get them to like you when you don't even like you. I didn't like who I was, so why would some random strangers? Because of this attitude and mindset, I really struggled with making friends when I was depressed. The funny thing is that having friends when you're feeling depressed can honestly help you improve. But when you're depressed you feel isolated, so it's kind of like its own self-fulfilling prophecy or cycle of doom. You need friends to feel better, but you can't make friends because you feel terrible, and so on in a cycle that seems to never end.

When I finally decided to make a change, I was able to slowly change my mindset. My pastor helped me with this process. When he invited me to let God help me heal, I started going to church again. If you go to church, you know how close-knit the whole community can be. People will welcome you in and in a very short time, you can find a group of people who click with you. When I started going to church, I eventually got connected with a small group and I started the slow process of making friends.

It's hard to make friends as an adult, not only because of the fact that we don't really just meet random people to be friends with like we do as children but also because of the level of vulnerability necessary in friendship. Good friendship, a good tribe, requires us to be vulnerable and to put ourselves out there to connect with one another. How else will we support each other?

So finding new friends requires a level of trust, not only in the random people you're talking to but also in yourself. It took a long time for me to have the necessary self-confidence to find a good group of friends. This is especially true because I didn't feel like I was worthy of having friends. I didn't feel like I was good enough for them yet. So I had to work on that aspect of myself before I could put myself forward as friend material. I had to trust myself to be a good friend, and then I could finally put things forward to make good friends.

When it's time to find new friends, really take the time to get to know them. These people will be your support group and you want to make sure that they're going to reflect positivity back at you, instead of echoing any negativity that's already going through your head. As you go about meeting new people, you're going to come across a lot of haters, especially if they know the struggles you're going through. Turns out, not everyone is nice to strangers. Who knew? As I said, it takes some vulnerability before you find friends who will have your back in tough times. It also takes a lot of trial and error. For every good person you'll meet, there are just as many who are not great friends. So pick and choose carefully.

One way I found friends who were supportive was by learning to identify my values and learning to find others who shared my values. Look at the things in your life that mean a lot to you. Think about your stance on public narratives, or how you what to be perceived. All of this can help you identify your values. Once you have them identified, you can use your values to help you find friends who share them.

Surround yourself with Like-Minded People

Being with friends who share your values is incredibly important, especially as you try to turn your life into something that you'll appreciate and love. For me, finding friends took a lot of time, but finding friends who shared my values took even longer. I learned to separate the friends who were good company, but not necessarily the ones I would share my dreams with, and the friends who were always emotionally there with you. I learned to create a supportive tribe of people who would be there for one another.

When you start to separate your friends into these categories, it can be a little awkward for you, but they don't need to know that you've put them in different categories when you're building a supportive community, you want to make sure that the people in that community are those who believe in you and will give you positive words, and even some criticism, without being negative. So look at your friend group and analyze how they are helping you or hindering you from reaching your goal.

Create a multi-tiered support system. What I mean by this is to choose supports from all over your life, not just from your friend group or family groups. Instead, find a combination of both, and maybe even include some people who are not in either group. I feel like friends are often more supportive than family members, at least in my situation. While I wouldn't rely on some of my immediate family for support, I would rely on my cousin for it any day of the week, and I would do the same for him. He's the one who helped me really notice that I had a problem and that I needed to get help for it. His loving attitude and his never-ending support put him firmly in the support group category, whereas some of my other family members wouldn't be invited to join that club.

So in your support group, choose people that you really feel safe around. If you have friends or family members who always give you kind encouraging words, and actually mean them, add them to your support group list.

Beyond just finding people who are going to love on you when you're down, and give you a helping hand when you need it, look for people who have a similar mindset to you, but maybe have different skillsets than you do. If your group of close friends is full of people who are just like you, then you're shortchanging yourself. You won't get to experience as much from a group of people who are identical to you, in comparison to having a varied group of friends who will challenge and encourage you. So, be with people who will support you, but will also present things from different perspectives, maybe perspectives you hadn't considered before. Have a good mix of people in your idea of a good support group.

When I say surround yourself with people who are like-minded, I mean find people who share your values even if they come from a different career, background, or have a different set of hobbies for you. If you are driven, find driven people. If you're positive or want to be more positive, surround yourself with positive people.

You've worked so hard to make it to your goals, and you've worked so hard to value yourself. You took the first step at some point and you know that you're enough. So you want to be around people who aren't going to set you back. You want to be with people who value themselves too, who know they're enough, and who are actively going for their goals. They don't want to settle or stay in their parent's dreams. They want more and they're driven to get more. Find people who care about progress and who will want to see you succeed. Find people who will help you just like you'll help them. And Find people who share your values, whatever those are.

Your goals are so much easier to achieve if you have these people in your life. With a tribe to support you, you can achieve nearly anything. For me, as I learned to take my first steps, set goals, and handle depression, I had to also find that support group. Church gave me a readymade group of friends who were somewhat like-minded, but even then, I had to look for the people who were going to be the ones I would contact no matter what. That took time and a lot of effort. Eventually, I found them. I also eventually found a group of great people online who shared a mindset similar to my own and who are always so supportive of each other. This was so important to me because I had always felt belittled by my family or peers when I was growing up, so having adult relationships where people were supportive is amazing.

When you put together your group of supportive people in your mind, find people who are going to be there to talk about fresh ideas. Find people who want to explore new and interesting topics, who will bounce ideas off of you, and who will have conversations with you that will help everyone move forward. A good tribe won't belittle your goals, dreams, or ideas. A good tribe will offer you critical thoughts, but also kind criticism to help you improve your ideas. They'll help you refine your thoughts and improve yourself. They will challenge you to be your best! Find a tribe like that. You are worthy enough to have a tribe like that.

It's Okay to Ask for Help

When we're in the lowest parts of our lives, or really suffering under the burden of something, it can be so hard to ask for help. I feel like this is especially true for men. We've been taught to suffer on our own and to make it on our own, so when the time comes where we truly need help, we don't ask for it, even when there are people right there already offering their help.

We're not capable of doing everything on our own and asking for help doesn't make us weak. In a way, asking for help is a sign of strength. It's a sign of you understanding the value of your community and accepting that you aren't a perfect human specimen. Asking for help means that you're curious and willing to learn more. Asking for help means that you have the drive or passion to move forward, even if you can't do it on your own. Asking for help is a very smart, strong, move.

The thing is, that humans weren't designed to be the Lone Ranger. People always say that "no man is an island" and it's true. Our brains are set up to live in supportive groups because our brain knows that it's in groups that we're safe, and in groups that we learn. We're a part of a larger community of people around us, and this applies even if we choose to isolate ourselves away from others.

95

The sad thing is that this Lone Ranger mentality isn't one shared around the world. American culture prizes independence and we learn that independence from when we are young children. But around the world, there are cultures that prize community support more than independence. In most cultures beyond Western ones, community connection is far more important than going it alone. It isn't about individual praise, but rather about what a community can do together. Living in a country of independent, strong people who want to make it on our own is great, but it can also be much harder than it needs to be.

We often need the help of people around us to make it, to be better people, and to share ideas. A strong person asks for help, and gives help when it's needed. They put their independence and stubbornness to the side for a moment to get the help they need.

I had to do the same thing. I had to learn that it's okay to ask for help, to really reach with two hands for it, instead of suffering alone. I was in such pain that I literally thought about dying to escape that pain. But when I was finally ready to get help, it was right there and had been just waiting for me to ask. Getting help from that pastor and the psychologist were the best decisions I made, and they didn't make me weak. Working with them, I was able to get help to dig myself out of a hole and it made me stronger overall. It made me feel human again. Today, my friends and loved ones give me help and so too does my faith in God. Knowing that there's always someone there to lend a hand has changed my life for the better. It helped me to become stronger the moment I had those supports in place.

If we're friends and I ask you for help to move from one house to another, does that make me weak for asking? Absolutely not and it's normal to get help in a move. If I slip and fall on a hiking trail, and I ask for help walking back to the trailhead, does that make me weak? Nope. It's again a normal thing. Isn't it funny how asking for help with physical things is completely normal and acceptable in our culture, but asking for help for psychological or emotional things isn't? But we can change that. Asking for help in any area of our lives should be completely normal, and an accepted practice. I feel like we're getting there as a society. We're learning to accept that we all need help sometimes and that it's okay to ask for it. If you never hear that from anyone else, hear it here: it's okay to ask for help.

We can't ask for help until we become aware that we have a weakness. We have to be aware that we can't always do everything on our own, and that something that's making us struggle, doesn't have to be worked on alone. This is especially true for mental health issues. If you're struggling psychologically, reach out even though it's hard. Your tribe of true friends will be there to support you, but you can also ask for help from others who are not necessarily in your tribe.

They just have to be a safe and trustworthy person. For me, the pastor and psychologist were the people I felt were safe enough to reach out to. They were two people who I knew would keep my confidence and help me simply because their chosen profession demanded it. Yeah, it made me feel vulnerable to talk to strangers about such personal problems, but if I hadn't, I would be in the exact same spot I was in years ago, or I would be in a worse one. I was very lucky that the pastor I talked to was a good, ethical guy and that he was trustworthy. Some pastors aren't, but you won't know that unless you take a chance. Nearly every psychologist or mental health professional will keep your confidences and will support you no matter what. They'll help you get out of your hole and live a full life. So if you don't have a group of friends yet, like I didn't before, reach out to a person like this because they're safe, and they'll help you get better.

Each of us is on a journey in our life, and we're always going to come to a point where we need help. That's one hundred percent okay! We should never shame each other for needing help because we will all need it one day. Literally, every single one of us cannot make it alone. We will all need help at one point or another. Asking for help in your life is incredibly hard, and it can be a blow to your ego, but it's so incredibly important. If you're not asking for help, then you're going to be taking the hard road, and wasting your own time.

Connecting Lessons with Food

Lasagna

Ingredients:

- 2 Tbsp. Oil
- 1 lb. lean ground beef (or your favorite substitute)
- 1 Packet of Onion soup mix
- 1/2 tsp. Garlic powder
- ½ tsp sugar
- 1/2 tsp pepper
- 1 tsp. Oregano
- Salt to taste if desired
- 1-1/2 cups water
- 1- 6 oz. can tomato paste
- 1- 8 oz. can tomato sauce

Cook ½ lb. lasagna noodles, or try the uncooked version of noodles as mentioned below*. Noodles cook great and saves time and those steps to cook separate.

1 pound Ricotta or can substitute with cottage cheese

1 lb. Mozzarella cheese (shredded)

4 Tbsp. Parmesan cheese (shredded)

Heat oil in pan and add dry spices to blend flavors. Add meat and brown. If you use lean meat you don't have to drain the fat. Add water and stir in soup mix then add tomato paste and sauce. Use low heat to simmer for 25 minutes.

Prepare lasagna noodles according to package directions or *use uncooked noodles (add ¼ cup water if doing this) and layer as follows.

In a 12x8 cooking dish or pan: layer starting with noodles then meat sauce, next add cheese. Continue to layer until all ingredients are used up. Make sure to end with meat sauce and Mozzarella cheese as top layer. Sprinkle on Parmesan cheese. Bake at 350 degrees for 30-35 minutes. Cook uncovered.

Chapter Eight

Make a Code of Conduct

We're coming up to my final piece of advice, which is to make a code of conduct for yourself. It's easy to fall into patterns of thoughts and actions and those patterns are influenced by everything in our lives. But sometimes, to make a truly good change, we have to step back and define what we are to ourselves and what we want to be. Creating a code of conduct is a way to do this.

A code of conduct means looking at and defining what we want to do, in relationships, and in the words we choose to use. It's closely connected to our values and sets us up to succeed or fail. Take the time to reflect on the type of person you want to be and create your code of conduct. It took a while for me, but I now have several things that I do because I want to be that type of person. I want to make sure that I'm there to support people in a way that I wasn't supported growing up. So here is my code of conduct, and my recommendations for you to consider.

Always Treat Others Well

I think a large part of this comes from my faith and just my understanding of how God wants us to treat each other. In the Bible, there are repeated stories and parables about how we have to care for one another. It always explains the importance of treating others well, even if we don't agree with them. You can look at the stories like the one about the Good Samaritan, or nearly every action that Jesus Christ took as beautiful lessons on how to treat others well. Christ's focus was on treating others well and helping them achieve their everlasting life, but those are lessons we can repeat in our lives now.

We should treat each other with kindness because we often don't know what's happening in a person's life. We don't know what struggles they're going through or how they're suffering so we should treat each other well because who knows how our words and actions will affect someone who is already in a rough place. With an unkind word, we can push people into more destructive behaviors. But with a kind one, we can help people see that there's some good in the world. You never know if that one positive conversation or action may help them in the future. It could even save their life.

There's a story about a young guy who was really struggling with some mental health issues, and on the day he decided to die by suicide, he was riding the bus and he told himself that if just one person reached out to him, he wouldn't take his own life. So he waited just trying to see if someone would be kind to him, but no one was. He later jumped off the Golden Gate Bridge, and while he miraculously survived the fall, just think about how if someone had said a kind word, he wouldn't have jumped at all. So treat others with kindness and give them a kind word, even if they're a stranger you've never met before, and maybe won't ever meet again. It's amazing how much a simple kind word can help someone struggling heal a little.

I feel like we should treat others in kindness especially when they're not being kind to us. If someone is an ass to you, it's probably not you but a series of events that have happened in their life up to this point, and you're their outlet to let their frustrations loose. You don't know what they're going through or what difficulties they've faced earlier in the day and honestly, we've all had truly terrible days where we end up unleashing our rage on an unsuspecting person. If we can keep this lesson in mind when we're dealing with a person being an ass to us, then we can often step out of our own anger and respond to their words with kindness, instead of taking it personally. This will be an ongoing lesson for me. It's something I always want to do and though I may not be one hundred percent successful in all situations, if I can keep in mind that I can be kind in tough situations, then I'll make my own response better instead of taking their words personally.

We've all been there when someone has been so aggressive to us, far beyond what the situation calls for. When that happens, don't try to match their level of aggression or respond in kind because really, that just makes the situation worse. Instead, stop and listen to them. Listen to what they're actually saying and try to see if there's an underlying frustration they're going through, which is making them say these things. You could even just stop them with a simple and kind, "What's going on right now?" Because sure, you could be their problem, but nine times out of ten, it was a bunch of other stuff that happened and something finally broke the camel's back and you're there to receive this person's outburst. It's a series of things in this person's day, week, or month that has led to this aggressive moment and if you stop them with some kindness, and genuinely ask them what's happening, what's going on, most people will start to slow down. If you approach them by explaining that you don't understand what's happening or why they're angry in a kind, loving way, often the aggression will go right out of them because they've received kindness back, instead of further aggression. Talk with them about what's happening and what they're interpreting in the conversation and sit with them.

Communicate your kindness towards them and slow everything right down. In that way, you can connect with someone while also helping them calm down when they're having an aggressive moment.

We should treat each other with kindness because you get back what you put out in the world. This is a pretty common idea about what we put out, we receive right back. Karma if you will. If we are kind to people on a daily basis, all of a sudden it will become a habit that's easier and easier to reach out for. So kindness will be our first response, instead of our second or third response. And as we continue to act in kindness, then people will also start to act kindlier towards us. Remember, our brains are hardwired for social connection, so when we act in a positive way, that's what we receive in return, simply because it's the way our brain is set up. When we see someone's kindness, we want to be kind in return. Think about those awesome "pay it forward" actions. The person in front of you in a drive-thru line pays for your coffee. All of a sudden you also want to be just as kind, so you pay for the next person in line's coffee. That's how kindness

106

works. What you put out there in the world will go around, and it will often come right back to you in other ways. So be kind.

We should treat each other with kindness because acting out in pain causes you more harm than good to our self-perception. I think that just in general, if we approach life with some kindness, then we'll start to be kinder to ourselves too. If we can be kind to a friend, or a stranger, then we can also learn to be kinder to ourselves. And that's okay. I know that for a lot of people, myself included, we learned that being kind to ourselves and connecting with our emotions wasn't a positive thing. My dad taught my brother that real men don't cry. But that's not true. We should connect with our emotions and share those emotions with others. By learning to accept our emotions and experience them, we can learn to be kinder to ourselves, just as we're kind to others.

Treating other people well can honestly change your life. You can all of a sudden make connections with new people, and have a legacy leftover. When you walk away from a situation where you treated someone well, they're going to remember that and they'll remember your kindness, even if they were rude in return. That will create a legacy that will follow you around, and all of a sudden, you'll be That Guy. That guy who always has a kind word or kind action. It will define you and will turn you into a safe person for people to talk to. So treat others well, like you would want to be treated on the worst day of your life.

Take Care of Yourself

It's so important to treat others well, but it's just as important to treat yourself well and to take care of yourself. After all, you can't keep giving from a dry well. You can be so kind, or even too kind, and give everything of yourself to other people but that can result in you just rolling over while they walk over you. So you also have to set your boundaries to help you take care of yourself too. Creating your boundaries is how you can take care of yourself. Without boundaries, you can often lose your sense of self-worth and forget your values in an attempt to please other people. All of a sudden, all of your personal values are based on how others perceive you, instead of how you perceive yourself, so set some boundaries and learn to remind people that you do have a limit.

Another thing you can do to take care of yourself is to start practicing self-care. In the media and on social media, self-care has been a buzz word for a long time, and that's because there's some actual truth to it. Self-care is a way to rejuvenate yourself and care for your needs so that you are in a better position to face your day or week. Self-care is a way to take care of you as an individual, without focusing on taking care of others. It means doing something just for yourself.

Your self-care actions could be as simple as eating three meals a day and going to bed at a good time. These two actions alone will help you live a good life, but you could always take it further. Self-care actions are about putting yourself first for a moment, so consider what are some things that you do that are just for you, not for everyone else. And if you don't have an answer to that thought, then maybe it's time to find a little more self-care in your life.

You can go out and purchase self-care products if you want to, but you don't have to do that (remember, you want to become addicted to saving, not buying the latest bath bomb). Self-care doesn't require additional products; all it requires is your presence. For me, some actions I take for self-care is playing with dogs, reading the bible, and taking time to reflect on my life. Even cooking, which I often do for others, can be something I do for myself as an act of self-care. Another self-care thing I do for myself is not watching the news. I find that the negativity in the news on TV is just so hard to get through and it will bring my day right down. So by avoiding watching the news, I'm taking care of my psyche and myself.

Consider adding self-care activities to your own life. Activities like meditation, exercising, sitting in silence, praying, or just going for a walk in nature can help you reduce your stress, and give you a sense of reset. Even doing something simple like not checking your social media feed first thing in the morning can be an act of self-care, especially if that drama early in the day creates a rough day for you.

Self-care is helpful because it gives you a fresh start and sets you up for being able to create new things and solve problems. When you feel rejuvenated from self-care, you're more likely to be motivated to do other things in your day. It can also help you become more productive later on and give you a fresh start to your creativity. So taking some time for yourself in your day is an excellent way to take care of yourself beyond meeting your basic needs. So take care of yourself through setting boundaries and also by doing some self-care activities.

Give Encouragement to Others

This concept often goes hand in hand with treating others with kindness, but I also feel like it's a little different. We treat others with kindness with our words or actions, but giving encouragement is a little more active. It requires us to connect with people and genuinely consider their value, and then reinforce that value to them.

Giving people encouragement can be a great way to remind them of just how important they are to you. It can also be a great way to add some positivity into their own lives and into your life too. I remember not feeling encouraged through a large portion of my adult and young adult life. There were some consistent people in my life who provided encouragement and gave me the will to keep going and keep trying, but I always think more encouragement isn't a bad thing.

Think about a time in your own life, when a word of encouragement could have made the difference between you going for what you wanted, or sitting back and waiting. Since that happened to me, I now try to make a point of encouraging people and giving them just a little dose of positivity.

Be Grateful

It doesn't matter how hard your life is or how much you're struggling. If you can find a moment to be grateful for something, even the tiniest thing, it can help improve your mental health and give you a dash of positivity. Being grateful for things has been shown to really improve our mental health, our self-love, and change the way we treat others. We can all find something in our lives to be grateful for, even when things are tough.

The truth is, that everything that has happened in my life up until this moment led me here. And where I am right now, is a good place. So even though my past has had a lot of pain and hurt, failed chances and missed opportunities, it still brought me to this moment. It helped me grow and develop as a person and it helped me define who I am and who I want to be. So I have to be grateful for my past, even though at the time it was something truly horrible for me.

I can be grateful for the things I learned and accept those hard lessons as something that turned out positively, instead of something that is always negative. If I can learn to appreciate and accept a setback, not as a failure but as a lesson for something else in my life, then I can carry the positive mindset into other areas of my life.

Each moment in my life brought me to this moment, so I have to be grateful for those life lessons. If things hadn't been so rough for me in the past, I wouldn't have learned how to successfully cope with pain and I wouldn't have grown in resilience and strength. Perhaps most importantly, I wouldn't have gained faith like I have right now.

I'm so grateful for my faith in God and how it's absolutely changed my life. It's healed me and changed my perspective on so many things. Without it, I wouldn't be where I am today, but I wouldn't have gotten to the point of accepting faith if it wasn't for all of those hard times in my life before. I feel like, throughout my life and even now, there have been so many God moments that taught me something new or completely changed my perspective. Those moments helped to ease my struggles a little and helped my life to get a little better. So I'll always be grateful for how my life brought me to God and how God and my faith later kept my life moving forward.

We can also be grateful for the people we've met on the journey who have helped us thrive. Friends, pastors, psychologists, cousins, moms, grandmas, and so on have all in some way influenced my life for the better and I'm so grateful for that. Without these people in my life, I would be an entirely different person. Pain, ultimately led me to this moment right now, where I've grown as a person and changed myself to be someone who is kinder than he was. Life lessons taught me how to care for others, and I can be grateful for that.

Learning to feel grateful for all the pieces of your life can lead to a fulfilled life. It can create greater connections with people and our community. And yes, being grateful for the hard, terrible things in your life is hard, but it can also be a way to forgive your past self or past people who hurt you by changing how you frame them.

Gratitude is so much more than learning to appreciate what has happened in your life. It has benefits that carry over into every aspect of your life. Practicing gratitude can impact your life physically, psychologically, and socially, all in a positive way.

Physically, practicing gratitude can surprisingly impact your body. When we practice gratitude, we are taking a mindful moment, this impacts the way our body runs. With less stress and anxiety, our bodies can heal faster with a better immune response. Our blood pressure goes lower and we're more likely to go out and experience other things. Practicing gratitude can even affect our sleep.

While the physical benefits are amazing, it's the psychological and social benefits that are really fascinating to me. When I was depressed, I would have been hard-pressed to find things to be grateful for, but if I had tried, I would have found that finding as little as three things to be grateful for in a day would have helped relieve some of my symptoms of depression. There are so many studies out there that support this. Being grateful improves and increases the level of positive emotions we feel, and that in turn reduces our levels of depression and anxiety, which in turn gives us physical benefits like better sleep and an improved heart rate. So it's a cycle that feeds itself and can improve our lives in so many ways.

Socially, being grateful means that I can connect with people in a more positive way. Being bitter about the sour grapes life had dealt me will only lead to bitter reactions with people, and really ruin any chance to build up relationships. But if I'm grateful and have a more grateful heart, I can learn to forgive and have more positivity in my reactions with other people. Being grateful makes people more compassionate towards each other, and more likely to forgive slights or mistakes. This in turn helps to build stronger relationships that will help to reduce feelings of loneliness or isolation. Avoiding loneliness and isolation means that I can also reduce those feelings when I feel depressed. So again, it all affects each aspect of our lives.

For me, practicing gratitude helped me adjust my mindset too. It helped me step away from negative thoughts and improve my positive self-talk. So instead of focusing on how terrible I was at things or how unworthy I felt, I was able to think about the things I could do that I was grateful for. I'm grateful for the fact that I can see, even with an eye injury. I'm grateful for the fact that I can and have learned from my mistakes and created a life for myself that I now enjoy. Having these positive thoughts about myself helped me to change my self-perception and regularly reminding myself of the way I'm grateful for things really led to a positive change in my life.

So being grateful for things can have an overall positive impact on our lives. But how do we go about practicing how to be grateful? There's a lot of good advice out there, and you could just spend time in the morning reflecting on the things

115

you're grateful for each day. But you could also try other things that fit you better. For me, looking back on my life and remembering how bad things were helps me feel grateful for where I'm at now, and how those bad things led to a positive outcome. However, if that brings you down and starts you in the process of rumination, then don't use that as your way to becoming grateful. Instead, find other means.

Keeping a gratitude journal is an easy way to practice gratefulness. A gratitude journal is just a place where you write a couple of things you're grateful for every day, even if you're having a truly terrible day. No matter how good or bad your day is going, I can guarantee that you can find something positive in your life that you're grateful for. Pets, loved ones, even having your basic needs met can all count towards gratitude, and if you write the same things over and over again, that's okay too.

There are so many ways we can practice gratitude, simple things like telling people how much we appreciate them, or saying a simple thank you once someone has done something for us. Just find a way to express your gratitude to reap the benefits in your life.

Never Hold a Grudge

There are a lot of people in my life, and a lot of events that caused me significant pain and suffering. Now, I could keep wallowing in what those people did or what happened with those events, but it won't do me any good. In fact, it will do a lot of harm. Choosing to hold on to a grudge means that you're choosing to stick with a negative mentality. It also means that you're choosing to relive the past over and over again. It can create a feeling of massive weight on you and holds you back emotionally from moving on in your life. Being stuck in a loop of a grudge forever is a great way to stay in a bad situation longer than you need to.

It's so easy for our lives to become consumed by what was done for this. Psychologists often call this rumination, where we end up just going over the negative events in our life over and over again, never letting them go and never healing from them. But where does that put us? It puts us exactly back where we started, and instead of healing from our wounds, we end up just picking the scab and reopening wounds that should have healed a long time before.

So it's always best to let a grudge go. It's something that I'm trying to live by and though it can be hard, honestly setting aside my grudges has helped me move on. It's also given me the space to learn lessons from past hurts and apply those lessons to my current and future behavior. I cannot live my life consumed by things that happened to me. Even with my brother, I had to learn to let the past go. There was a point where I hadn't talked to him for a long time, like I didn't with my dad, just to keep the peace. Eventually, though, we reconciled a little. We were at my cousin's house, and this was just before my brother passed. But during that conversation, we talked about the hurts that happened to both of us and how we could turn that hurt into something positive, by letting it go. We didn't have to let it consume our lives. While I'm not sure if he took this idea to heart or not, I really wish that I had had more time to talk with him about it.

Don't let your past hurt become an obsession you keep alive today. Let it go so that you can start to heal and grow from your experiences. Letting go of a grudge and learning to forgive are so important, doctors often talk about it. From a mental health standpoint, learning to forgive and let things go is important to our wellbeing, but it also has a physical aspect. If we are constantly reliving the stress of negative events and hold on to pain, it affects our stress levels and can even increase our blood pressure. So to help you take care of yourself, learn to let go of grudges and move on with your life.

It's important to recognize that letting go of a grudge doesn't mean that I condone the actions of people who hurt me. I still think that what they did was terrible, but I can accept that it happened and choose to move on with my life, instead of giving them ongoing power over my life and wellbeing.

Let Your Light Shine

By this I mean be comfortable with who you are and what you're capable of doing, then share that with other people. Be who you are and don't apologize for it. Be comfortable with what you have to offer the world, and then actually go out and offer it. Use the talents that you have to make the world a better place and be proud of those talents. It leads to a brighter, happier life.

Given the opportunity, I like to help people when I can, and I know where my talents lay. One time, our church was looking to build a new dining facility for a summer camp hall. This was up in the mountains of Montana and they were looking for people to come up and help finish the drywall. I called the supervisor and offered to do it since I had the tools already and the experience. The camp direct later spoke about how helpful it was and how grateful he was that I stepped up and offered a helping hand.

This is letting your light shine. By using my talents and skills to help others, I was able to share them with others. It helped me feel good about myself, but also showed others what I valued and what I was worth. Because I didn't hide what I could do, I was able to help make a difference in the community. So sharing what you can do with your community is so very important. After all, you'll be lending a helping hand to people and help build up your community at the same time.

Sometimes, we're taught to hide our talents and skills, or we want to selfishly hoard them. That's a choice, but I think it's not the greatest choice. After all, we are meant to help one another, so if you have the skillset to do that, why not help? Unless of course, it violates your own boundaries, which we discussed earlier in this section.

I think that for many people, if you suppress your talents and skills, or your goals and targets, you end up settling for what you have now, instead of aiming for what you could have. It dims your light and then one day, it will be gone altogether. When that happens, it will take a lot of work to find that passion again. That's what happened to me. I eventually learned to really hide what I wanted and I didn't set new goals. So I got more and more depressed until my light was so dim, I couldn't find it anymore. It took an act of God, and love and help from others to manage to find my passions again and to be confident enough to share them with others. Don't let your light dim just to feel more comfortable or to settle. Live your light and use it to help others.

My current passions are all about food and so that's the light I'm choosing to shine. I got into the whole experience after being a part of a great community. Having friends and supporters who are like-minded and ultimately confident in what I could offer, helped me feel more confident in what I could offer the world. Of course, this came after I lost my way a little and after I lost my focus on previous targets, but I eventually came up with using cooking as a way to let my light shine. Cooking was a way to help me stay sane during the winter times in Montana, and it was something I reached for after working on cars as part of my hobby. But cooking builds up others just as much as it builds up me. It helped me connect with my community in a way that I couldn't before. So all of a sudden, I was able to combine passions by doing multiple things I enjoyed and helping the community in the same breath. It was like catching two birds with one seed. I was able to go to car shows and instead of just sharing the car I built, I was able to cook there and share food with others, creating a stronger community and talking about the awesome cars around us. Bringing the community together around favorite things was one of my newest passions and it's something I want to keep maintaining for years to come.

I let my light shine in ways I wasn't expecting, but it enriched my life and made me feel fulfilled. So I recommend you look at what you can offer and then go do that. Share what you have to give with the community and you'll be amazed at the connections you can make and just how supportive everyone around you is.

Learn to Say No

This is a part of setting boundaries, but it's so important to know when to say no. You can't give everything that you have to others, or else you won't have anything left for yourself. But it takes a lot of effort to say no to others. For me, this is especially true because I do like helping people, but sometimes I can't or sometimes I find that people will walk right over me, relying on me to fix all of their problems when they need to work on it themselves. So I had to learn to say no.

I've always been a yes person. Someone can ask, "Hey can you do this," and my answer was always yes. And I would go do it, often to my own detriment. I mean, I would often put money into other people's things out of kindness or a wish to please them, but it was hurting me in the long run. I think for a while, people loved me just because I was helpful and I cultivated that because in the past I couldn't really figure out how else to get people to love me. By pleasing people, I was able to feel useful and loved, even when I was being used to complete things they didn't want to do or financial support things they didn't have the money for. But I had to learn how to say no and set my own boundaries.

One day at church years ago, there was this deal going on and this woman at the church asked me to do something for her. She was always asking me to step in and do this or that, but she often then turned around and talked about me and others negatively. So when she asked for this new thing, I decided that it was time to set up and say no. She kind of chuckled at me and then immediately asked me to do something else. I answered with no once again. She was shocked. She asked how could I say no, how could I do this?

But really, it was necessary for my own well-being. It was probably the first time in my life that I said no and followed through with it. I was forty-seven years old and I finally learned how to set my own boundaries. I stopped letting people take advantage of me.

Saying no means that you can focus on the things that really matter to you. For me, I still love helping people, but now I do it in a wise way, in a way that helps build up the community while still taking care of my own needs. If you're struggling with being a yes person like I was, then really take the time to reflect on why that is. I used saying yes as a means to confirm my worth, but it didn't actually do that. It just opened the door for people to take advantage. Now when I say yes, it's because I actually want to do that thing and I think it will be fulfilling for me. So why do you say yes, when you might actually want to say now? Reflect on that, and then maybe start practicing setting your boundaries and learning to say no.

Face Conflict

When I was a kid, I felt like my brother didn't like me very much. He was a scrapper, just like my dad, real tough. I didn't want to get my ass kicked by him, so instead of standing up for myself, I would just say, okay or I would walk away. As I got older there are many times where I didn't stand up when I should have. It reinforced this idea that I wasn't enough.

Of course, walking away from a fight doesn't mean I wasn't good enough or cowardly, but that's how I considered it for a long time. Coming from a negative lens, I thought that walking away was giving up my power and that the right thing to do was to fight back. However, I've come to realize that walking away is just as powerful as fighting and takes more strength.

But I've also learned that there's a time to step up and confront conflict. Even if I would prefer not to. Sometimes we've got to step up and take responsibility for a situation for the good of other people. So if you see someone struggling, help them. Stand up for them. And at the same time, stand up for yourself. Be like a brick wrapped in velvet. Show love and empathy, compassion. But be solid and strong underneath that.

Facing conflict and choosing to engage with it is another way you can reinforce your boundaries. If someone is doing something to you that violates your values, stand up to them. Say no, as I mentioned before, or simply take a stance. Explain your boundaries, or don't, but whatever you do, don't let someone push you into a corner you don't want to be in. Now hopefully, if you've worked on exploring your own values and really finding some compassion for yourself, then this won't be too hard, but if you're still struggling with identifying who you are and what you want, then standing up to conflict can be so very difficult. Keep practicing and use your tribe, your support group, to help you through it. With each conflict you face, the more confident you will become in your belief that you can handle most problems.

Wrap Up

To conclude this chapter, these are values and behaviors that I want to maintain in my life. Knowing that this is how I want to interact with the world gives me a very clear code of conduct that I can use in every interaction and every goal I set for myself. I recommend that you create your own code of conduct so it's always there like a rock, ready to support you when you might lose your way. And as with everything else in life, adapt your code of conduct to your life's circumstances and keep growing and developing.

Connecting Lessons with Food

Grilled Ribeye Steak

Ingredients:

- 1" to 1.5" thick cut Ribeye steak (best with bone in)
- 1-Tbsp Montreal Steak seasoning
- 1-Tbsp Johnny's seasoning salt

Season steak on both sides and edges as well

Heat grill using lump charcoal

Cook over medium heat either directly or indirectly over coals to your desired level using an instant read thermometer.

Here you have the choice to sear at the beginning of the cook or at the end.

You can use a cast iron pan to sear or use the grill and sear at the end.

If you sear at the end, remove from heat just short of your desired internal temperature, crank the heat up to about 500+ degrees then return the steak to the grill. Be VERY careful as it will start to flare up as the fat gets hotter and drips into the grill. Use long handle tongs and gloves to protect yourself. If you are unfamiliar with this method, research it ahead of time. There are some great videos on youtube to watch but pay attention to the flare up danger.

It may take a few times to get this perfected but hey, you get to eat all of the research!!!

It's best to start with the thinner cut if you are not very experienced.

My favorite method of cooking is on a Big Green Egg!!!!

Conclusion

Our personalities and our self-perception are not set in stone. We can grow and develop our understanding of ourselves so that we can have more confidence in our capabilities. This book has been an exploration of the lessons I've learned that helped to change my self-perception. No one has the perfect mindset right out of the gate, but all of us can take action to change our beliefs so that we can go for our goals and dreams. We can change our lives for the better, so long as we learn to accept ourselves and act with both self-love and compassion for others.

We often have an idea of who our true self is. This is the person you are right now. Not the person you were last year, or even the idealized version of yourself. It's who you are now. However, our true self is often buried under our negative self-talk, which sends us messages that go against the reality of who we are. Whether we tell ourselves that we are special and perfect, or whether we tell ourselves that we are nothing, worthless, we're wrong. Our self-perceptions can criticize us or inflate our egos, but we have to be aware of the self-talk so that we can see ourselves as we are.

If we believe that we're not smart enough, then this can be habitual, and it can be very hard to change habits. For most of my life, I used my negative self-talk to echo negative words thrown at me. I let it dominate my life and take away opportunities to grow. To make a change in my life I had to change my self-story and that only happened by being my own ally. By recognizing that I had a problem and I wasn't ready to give up on life, I stood up for myself and my well-being.

I was lucky enough to have support from others around me, but even without that support, we need to support ourselves and be self-compassionate. We have to be aware of the negative self-talk and be prepared to combat the beliefs we've carried all our lives.

It's a lot harder than it seems like it would be, to change these negative habits. It took me years and years to finally get to this point, where I change my first negative thought into something more hopeful and positive. Something that can help end negative thoughts is to imagine that you're saying these words to someone who is your friend. You wouldn't tell your friend who is struggling that they're garbage, worthless, or not enough, right? So don't do that to yourself. You can also think of it in the opposite direction. If you're struggling with negative self-talk, think about a good friend and what they would tell you during this tough time. Think of a friend who will give you stories of compassion and empathy. They won't offer false promises, but they do offer support through thick and thin. They provide you with compassion and empathy. They're not going to put you down when you fail. Instead, they might tell you that you'll do better next time. Even if you don't have a friend like this, you can be that type of friend to yourself.

Self-compassion can be the first step for changing your self-story and mindset. This can help you change your beliefs and actions so that you're kinder to yourself. Once you have more self-compassion, you may find yourself starting to believe in your ability to overcome challenges, and once you believe that, it will be easier to go out and achieve your goals.

The point I want to make with all of this is that it's never too late to turn your life around. It's never too late to learn more self-compassion and to change your life for the better. It's never too late to create goals and go for them. It's never too late to add more flavor to your life. Look at my own story for proof of this. It wasn't until I was in my forties before I started making the changes that brought me to this point.

And now here I am. I've come almost full circle, from loving food when I was a child to now experiencing the joy of serving food to others. While cooking wasn't always a part of my life, it's something that has added a wonderful spice to everything I now do. And it all started with making that first change when I was in my forties and seeking help from others.

I love watching people eat and enjoying the food I cooked. I like to sit back and eat last, just so I can see people enjoying themselves. This also gives me the chance to reflect on how my life has changed and how I reached this point. I really wouldn't have gotten as far as I have without the loving support of the community and I feel like food is the way I can share that back with the community.

I feel like food is the glue that holds people together. As we gather to eat, we connect with each other. We sit and are comfortable with one another, part of a community whether we are talkers or whether we are shy. And at the end of the day, when people come up to me and tell me how good the food is, well, there's nothing that can beat that.

Food brings people together. We build rapport with one another over food and it helps us start the process of building a relationship with another person, whether or not we ever see that person again. Food helps create memories and maybe it can even inspire someone to try something new too. Food can connect us with each other, even when we're hurting.

It's been a long road to get me here to this point, but I'm grateful for all the lessons I've learned. I'm hopeful that my actions now, and the things I put out in the world will help others also improve their life. This was part of the goal of writing this book, and I hope in some way that it's helped you find and recognize areas in your life that you want to change. Thank you for taking the time to read this, and I hope whatever you take away from this, you remember to love yourself, take care of yourself, and turn that back out into caring for the community.

Connecting Lessons with Food

Venison Biscuit Casserole

Ingredients:

- 2 Lbs. ground venison
- 1- 15 oz. can whole kernel corn
- 1- 14 oz. can dice tomatoes with juice
- 1- 4 oz. can of tomato sauce
- 1- cup shredded cheddar cheese
- 1- medium onion diced ¼"
- 2- Tbsp. Chili powder
- Salt and pepper to taste
- ½ stick melted butter
- ¼ cup cornmeal
- ½ green bell pepper diced
- 1- 15 oz. can green beans
- 1- can store bought biscuits

Brown the meat with onions in a large frying pan and add chili powder, salt and pepper.

In a greased three-quart casserole dish add the browned meat and onions and add tomatoes, tomato sauce, corn, cheese, bell pepper.

134

Mix all these ingredients and place in pre-heated oven for 10 minutes.

Melt the butter and roll biscuits in it, place them on top of the casserole, sprinkle with cornmeal and return to oven for 20-25 minutes or until the biscuits are golden brown.

Beef Stroganoff

Ingredients:

- 2 lbs. Round steak
- Salt and pepper to taste
- 1 medium to large onion (diced 1/4")
- 2- cans Cream of Mushroom soup
- 2- cans Cream of Chicken soup
- 1-1/2 cups of all-purpose flour
- 3 Tbsp. vegetable oil

Cut steak into 1" cubes, roll meat in flour then brown in frying pan with oil.

Cook until most of the pink is cooked through. Then place cooked meat into large casserole dish and set aside.

In the same frying pan add the diced onion, salt and pepper and cook for 1-2 minutes over medium heat, then add both kinds of soup and add 1 full can of water. Cook until heated through and mixed thoroughly then pour over meat and stir.

Bake at 375 degrees for approximately 90 minutes

Turkey Dressing

Ingredients:

- 1- Loaf of bread, white or wheat (cubed into 1" pieces)
- 4- large eggs (beaten)
- Salt and pepper to taste
- 1 ½ Tbsp. Poultry seasoning
- 2- Medium onions chopped and diced (1/4")
- 1- Cube of butter (8 Tbsp.)
- 2-cups of boiling water

Melt butter and partially cook onions and add seasonings.

In large container combine bread cubes, cooked onions, eggs, salt, pepper and poultry seasoning.

Blend all ingredients and add small amounts of the boiling water and mix with large spoon.

Mix until all ingredients are moist and blended well.

Place in baking dish and cook at 350 degrees for 1 hour. Cook to internal temperature of 165 degrees.

Mom's Tater Salad

Ingredients:

- 4- Large Potatoes (cooked and diced to 1" pieces)
- 3- Hardboiled eggs
- 1- Medium chopped onion (1/4" dice)
- Salt and pepper to taste
- Miracle Whip- start with 1 cup
- 1 Tbsp. prepared mustard

Mix mustard and miracle whip and thin with milk

Combine all ingredients and mix then chill one hour before serving

Mom's Fried Chicken

Ingredients:

1 full chicken separated or package of chicken legs/thighs. Leave skin on.

Wash well and pat dry with paper towels

Roll in flour (can add additional spices if desired)

Melt Crisco or butter in your favorite pan and just enough to keep the bottom of the pan wet

Arrange chicken in pan, try to keep a small gap between pieces if possible, ok if not

Cook on medium low to medium heat for 45 minutes to 1 hour

Turn pieces 1 time to get desired doneness and level of brown crust

Use instant read thermometer to verify chicken is cooked to at least 165 Degrees internal temperature

Remove from pan and let rest, loosely cover with aluminum foil

To make gravy:

Set heat to approx. Medium. Use a 3 Tbsp flour and mix in with drippings. (may get a bit crumbly) Adding slowly while stirring to minimize getting lumpy.

Cook until flour starts to brown then add milk starting with 1 cup.

Add seasoning to taste and keep stirring constantly

If lumps form stir rapidly and they can be mashed with fork or spoon.

Quinoa and black bean salad

Ingredients:

- 2/3 cup cooked Quinoa (cooled)
- 2/3 cup Black beans (rinsed and drain)
- 1 whole Avocado (mashed)
- 1 hardboiled egg (sliced)
- 3 Tbsp. Rotel tomatoes
- 2 Tbsp. Red Pepper Hummus
- Balsamic vinegar to taste. (I found that a 25-year-old Balsamic vinegar makes a much better flavor)
- Salt and pepper to taste

Prepare Quinoa according to package directions. Rinse and drain black beans. Cut open Avocado and remove pit. Scoop avocado from peel and mash.

Combine all the ingredients in a mixing bowl and refrigerate for 20 minutes.

Serve chilled and enjoy! Also great with crackers, your favorite bread slices, or fresh vegetables as a side dish.

Spaghetti Sauce

Ingredients:

- 1 & 1/2 lbs. Hamburger
- 1/2 lb. Italian sausage
- 1 whole onion chopped (medium size)
- 1- 32 oz. jars of Ragu Extra Spicy Sauce
- 1- 15 oz. can whole peeled tomatoes (Italian seasoned)
- 1- 16 oz. cans Cajun spiced tomatoes
- 2- 6 oz. cans mushrooms (if desired)
- 1- 6 oz. tomato paste
- ¼ tsp Cayenne pepper
- ¼ tsp Black pepper
- ¼ tsp white pepper
- ¼ tsp Oregano
- 2 Tbsp. Olive oil

Heat Olive oil in stock pot, add prepared onions and spices on low medium heat until onions start to soften. Add the Italian sausage and hamburger and brown the meat.

Once meat is browned, add remaining ingredients over low medium heat until heated through then reduce heat to simmer.

Let sauce simmer at least 1 hour stirring occasionally

Serve over your choice of Spaghetti noodles

This recipe goes great with garlic bread!

Thank You

Most importantly to God my Savior. You knew me before I was born. What my journey would be and when I would finally answer to your calling on my life. The words I look most look forward to hearing in the future are, "Well done good and faithful servant. Welcome to Heaven."

To my parents but especially my mom as she and I survived some terrible times together and were both made much stronger for it.

To my extended family, thank you all for holding that special place in my heart, the great memories and fun we have had along the way.

To those family members and friends called home way too soon, the memories of you all are so special.

To my lifelong best friends, Marty Krueger, Tim Melander, Howie Adams, Shawn Norick and John Babcock. John, who was my idol growing up and the man that I credit for saving my life when I was in my early teens through those insanely difficult painful years. You all have been there with me through the best and worst times of my life, those times I really needed you. Thank you.

To Ron Kinyon, the most talented man I know. Thank you for being my friend and being so patient with me during incredibly hard times. You are the person who taught me it was ok to make mistakes and keep moving on.

To Ed Mylett, thank you for the post you made on fb where you were standing on the beach talking about #Maxout, the very first time I heard that term. It was, in part about being the hardest worker in the room and how to demand better from ourselves. I have learned so much from you and all that you share with the world and I feel so blessed to be a small part of. For creating Arete with Andy Frisella. You two men have created the most amazing gift to help others.

To Tony Whatley and his amazing, beautiful wife Lisa, for being so kind, genuine and having the deep compassion and drive to help others reach destinations in our lives that we never could have imagined.

To Susanne Zavelle, for sharing the difficult times in your life on that first zoom call. That moment when you shared your personal struggles, immediately resonated with me and felt that instant bond that would lead to a lifelong friendship. I admire your strength and courage. That was the day I realized that. "I am enough." Those three words have launched me into a journey that quite literally has been life changing. Thank you.

Bio

I grew up on our family ranch in North Central Montana. We had most of the usual animals you would find in such an environment. My first three years of education were in the country school only two miles from my house, and yes we had to walk up hill both ways through 4 'snow drifts each and every day.

I attended that school until the start of my sophomore year when I moved to another school halfway across the state after my parents split up. I Graduated for Corvallis High School.

I tried a variety of jobs but most were seasonal so I joined the military then got medically discharged after a bad head injury that would change my life and the dream of becoming a helicopter pilot.

Florida was calling my name as that was one of the coldest winters here, we had in a long time. So, a buddy of mine and I packed our stuff in my little Honda Accord and headed south. It was 27 degrees the day we left in February that year. My dream was to get back to the water that I fell in love with a few years earlier. My next venture was to get involved in the Offshore Boat Racing scene and was blessed enough to do that very thing. During all these years of my life food was a constant love and passion for me as I was blessed to discover many incredible types of food.

Few things make me feel more happiness than to see people gather around food and enjoy each other's company. Due to missing my family I returned to the Pacific Northwest in Oregon to work with my brother in construction. That did not turn out to be the best thing, so I ventured on to find other work back in Montana.

Food became my focus and have enjoyed a lifelong passion to become a great cook and absolutely fell in love with real BBQ when I was in the south.

In the past years I rarely hear young people say things like, "I remember my grandma used to make...", or "my mom baked this...". These were of the best memories I have ever had when we used to gather for Sunday meals, picnics etc. It is becoming a lost art.

My new drive and passion are to help others make those memories and blessings weather the people included are blood related or not. I have four pillars to this passion. They are food, people, cars, and dogs. I want to help bring all these things together because so many are hurting in the world.

So, "Let's gather around the table" share stories, make memories and truly enjoy these blessings.

Made in the USA
Monee, IL
24 February 2021